UKULELE
Song Book
In Notation and Tablature
by Ron Middlebrook

Featuring:
Play 50 Popular Songs
arranged for easy playing
Learn:
Popular Strum Patterns
How To Tune

ISBN 978-1-57424-072-6

SAN 683-8022

Cover - Shawn Brown
Paste-up - Ken Warfield
Layout and Production - Ron Middlebrook

Table of Contents

How to Tune the Ukulele

**Few things sound as bad as an out of tune musical instrument,
so be sure your uke is in tune each time you begin to play.**

There are three ways to tune your ukulele:

Tuning with a uke pitch pipe
Tuning with a piano
Relative tuning

The tuning we use in this book is referred to as C tuning, which is the most widely used ukulele tuning (G-C-E-A).

All stringed instruments must be frequently re-tuned. You should tune your uke each time you play.

Tuning with a Uke Pitch Pipe

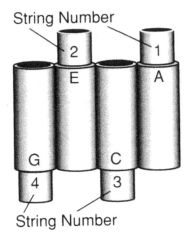

The pitch pipe is made up of four tuned pipes that coincide with the four strings of the uke. Blow lightly into the pipe and adjust the strings by turning the tuning keys until the sound made by the string is identical to the sound made by the pitch pipe.

The numbers indicate the string name from bottom to the top of the ukulele, as the uke is held in playing position.

Tuning with a Piano

Adjust the strings by turning the tuning keys until the sound made by the string is in the same pitch as the sound made by the piano.

Carefully tune as follows:

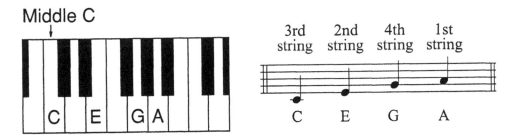

Relative Tuning

Whenever a pitch pipe, piano or another tuned ukulele is not available to you for tuning, the relative tuning method can be used. The following method will allow the uke to be in tune with itself, but not necessarily in tune with another instrument.

To tune up your uke with relative tuning:

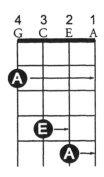

Turn the tuning peg of the 1st string (A) until it is fairly tight and produces a high tone.

Press the 5th fret of the 2nd string (E) and tune the 2nd string (E) to equal the pitch of the 1st string (A).

Press the 4th fret of the 3rd string (C) and tune the 3rd string (C) to equal the pitch of the 2nd string (E).

Press the 2nd fret of the 4th string (G) and tune the 4th string to equal the pitch of the 1st string (A).

Check your tuning each time you practice or play. Be sure your tuning pegs are tight. To keep the tuning pegs from slipping tighten the screws in the back of the pegs with a small screwdriver.

Holding the Ukulele

Keep both hands in an easy position without the slightest rigidity or strain upon any of the muscles.

The Left Hand

Place the tip of the thumb at about the center of the back of the Ukulele neck. Do not rest the neck of the Ukulele in the palm of your hand. Keep forearm and hand in an easy position. The fingers should curve naturally over the fingerboard and be able to press down lightly with the tips. Fingernails should be cut short, never allow the nails to come in contact with the strings as they have a tendency to cut them.

The Right Hand and Forearm

Let the middle of the forearm press the back edge of the ukulele to your body, holding it firmly but not too tight, so that you may be able to play either in a standing or sitting position.

Explanation of Strokes

There are many STROKES for the ukulele but the Common Stroke is the base or foundation for all.

The numerals 1,2, and 3 indicate the number of fingers used in the stroke and the U and the D indicate the up and down movements. When marked thus: 1/D means the up-stroke with one finger. When marked 3/D, it means a down stroke with three fingers.

The following strokes are suggested only, feel free to make up your own stroke to match the song.

The Common Stroke

A full round tone is best achieved by strumming the fingers at an angle to the upper part of the body of the Ukulele, this will bring the wrist directly above the sound hole.

The Stroke is made with the fore-finger of the right hand running it rapidly across all the strings with a down and up movement of the wrist, which must be perfectly free and keeping all the other fingers in readiness for another position. The down-stroke should be made squarely on the nail of the finger and the up-stroke with the fleshy part of the finger, but not on the side. There are two strokes to the beat, down and up. Make the down and up strokes even and smooth. Avoid jerkiness.

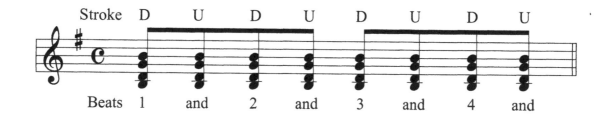

The Tremolo Stroke

This stroke is made in the same manner as the Common Stroke (down and up) but twice as fast. It must be played rapidly in order to produce a Tremolo effect.

The Triple Stroke

The stroke is made with the first finger only. There must be one stroke on the first, third and fourth beats, but the second beat demands three strokes, without interfering with the time.

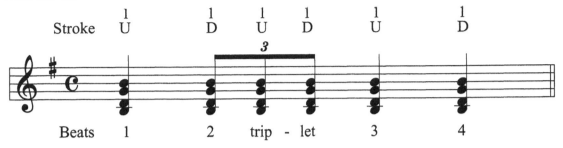

The Waltz Stroke

This stroke is made, first with the Up stroke of the thumb, followed by the first and second fingers about an inch apart.

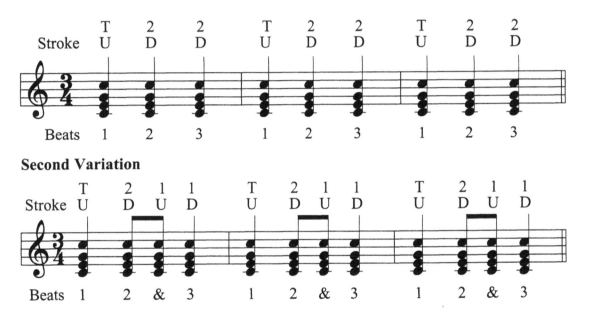

Tablature

All of the music in this book is written in standard musical notation and tablature. In tab, there are 4 lines, each representing a string on the uke. Numbers are placed on the lines corresponding to the frets on which you place your fingers.

Notes on the fretboard

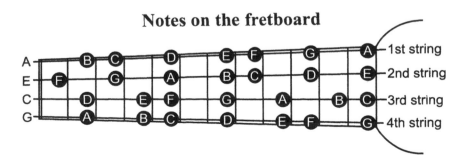

Roll Stroke

General Directions

The Roll Stroke is one of the most commonly used ukulele strokes and every good player should be able to use it properly. At the outset, the beginner may find his fingers a little stiff and clumsy but this disappears quickly after a little practice. There are only two steps to the Roll Stroke, but it is very important that each be mastered thoroughly. Start slowly and then gradually increase the speed of your fingers.

Start with Little Finger down (Fig. 1)

Start the little finger down across the four strings at the point where the neck joins the body. (See Fig. 1). It is very important that the down stroke be made on the fingernail. Otherwise the finger will catch and will not glide smoothly over the strings.

Figure 1.

Follow 1st, 2nd, and 3rd Fingers (Fig. 2)

Follow with the other three fingers as illustrated in Fig. 2. Bring all four fingers down across the four strings, making sure that the down stroke is one the fingernails. Practice going down across the strings with the fingers only again and again until you can do it smoothly.

Figure 2.

Then Follow Thumb (Figs. 3, 4, and 5)

As the forefinger leaves the last string, follow with the ball of the thumb down across all four strings. (See Figs. 3, 4, and 5). This completes the Roll Stroke. Practice the combination of the thumb and the four fingers until you can make one continuous stroke. You will find that the Roll Stroke can be worked in very effectively with the Triple Roll and the Common Stroke.

Figure 3.

Figure 4.

Figure 5.

Triple Roll

General Instructions

This is one of the prettiest of all ukulele strokes when properly executed. It is a very easy stroke, too, when analyzed. Follow the directions below, one step at a time. Master each step. Then practice the complete stroke at first very slowly. Then gradually increase the speed until you are producing a smooth continuous tone.

Bring First Finger Down

To start the Triple Roll, bring the forefinger down across all four strings at the point where the neck joins the body of the ukulele. Be sure to bring the finger down on the fingernail so that it will glide smoothly across the strings. Practice this part of the stroke again and again until you have mastered it thoroughly. (See Fig. 1)

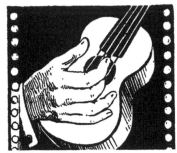

Figure 1.

Then Follow with Thumb Down

After the forefinger leaves the last string bring the ball of the thumb down across all four strings. (See Fig. 2). The thumb should follow the forefinger in one continuous stroke. Practice the combination of the forefinger and thumb until you can do it smoothly.

Figure 2.

Then Bring First Finger Up

As the thumb leaves the last string, bring the ball of fleshy part of the forefinger up across all four strings. (See Fig. 3). The forefinger should begin to go up the very second the thumb leaves the last string. This makes a continuous even stroke.

Figure 3.

Bringing the forefinger up and down once between each Triple Roll (See Figs. 4 and 5) can vary the Triple Roll.

Figure 4.

Figure 5.

Songs With 2 Chords

Songs With *2* Chords
Ain't Gonna Rain No More

Oh, it ain't gon-na rain no more, no more, it

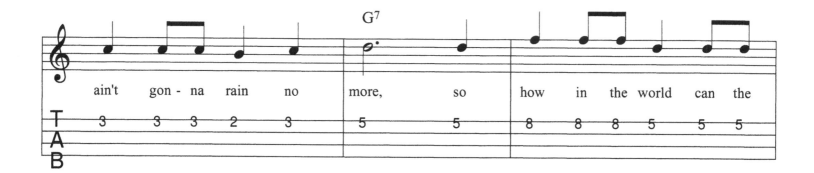

ain't gon-na rain no more, so how in the world can the

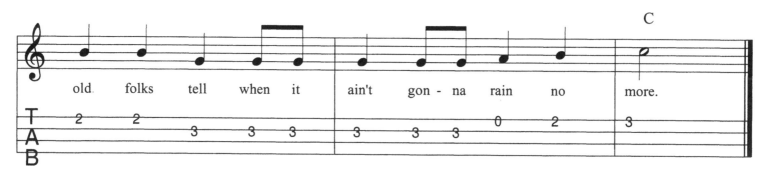

old folks tell when it ain't gon-na rain no more.

This arrangement © Centerstream publishing

Oh, a peanut sat on the railroad track,
It's heart was all a flutter,
A train came a roaring down the track,
Toot, toot peanut butter.

Buffalo Gals

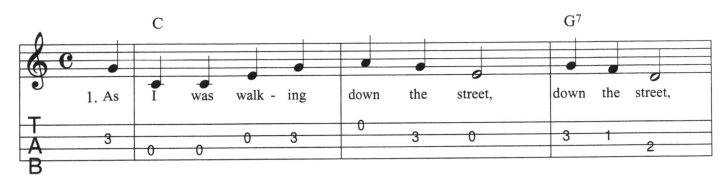

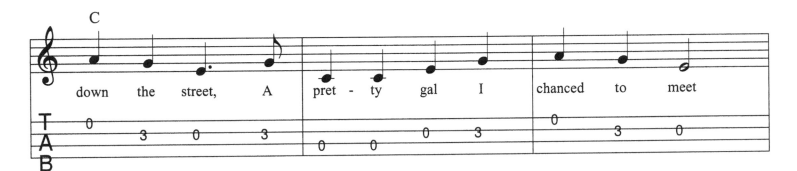

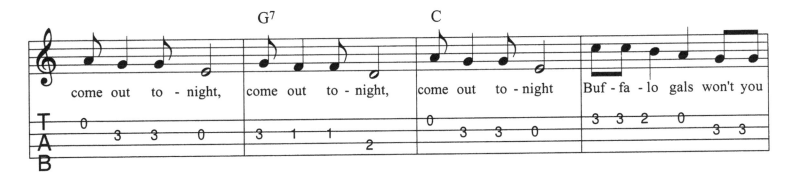

Clementine

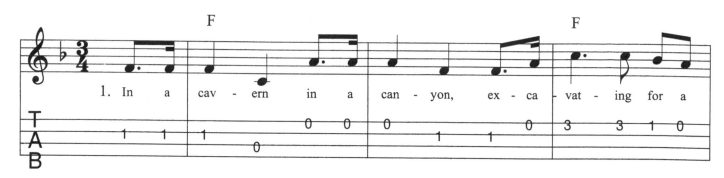

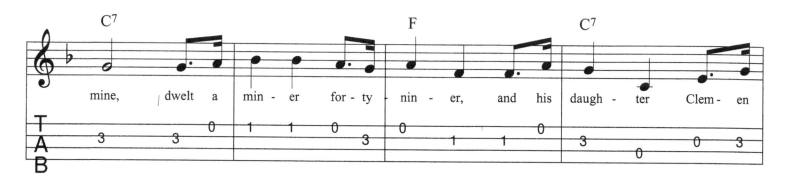

Chorus

2. Light she was and like a fairy,
   And her shoes were number nine,
   Herring boxers without topses,
   Sandals were for Clementine. *Chorus*

3. Drove she ducklings to the water,
   Ev'ry morning just at nine,
   Hit her foot against a splinter,
   Fell into the foaming brine. *Chorus*

4. Ruby lips above the water,
   Blowing bubbles soft and fine,
   But, alas, I was no swimmer,
   So I lost my Clementine. *Chorus*

5. How I missed her! How I missed her,
   How I missed my Clementine,
   But I kissed her little sister,
   I forgot my Clementine. *Chorus*

Down In The Valley

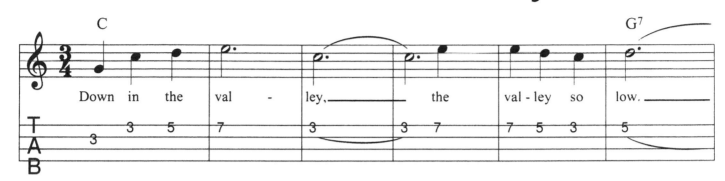

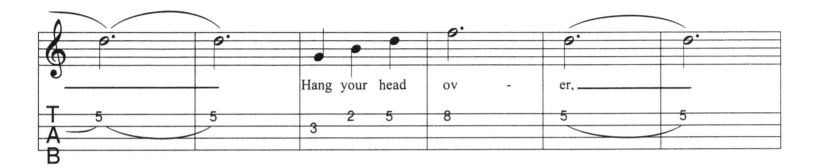

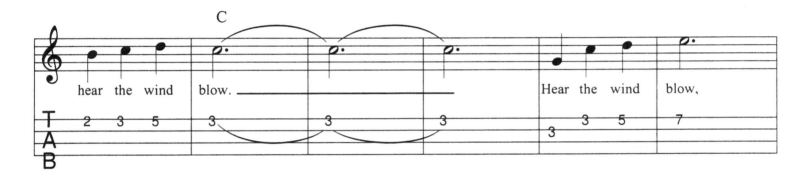

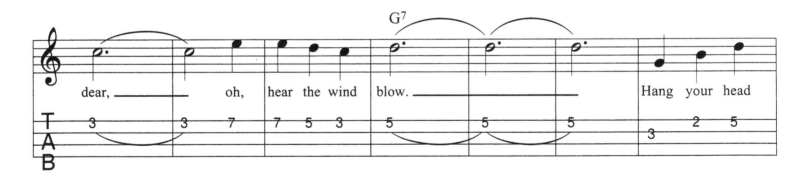

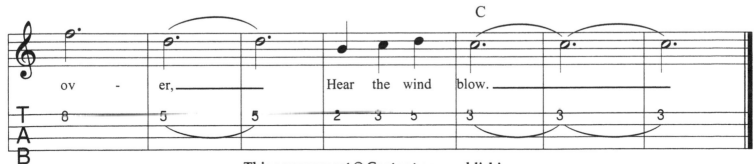

He's Got The Whole World

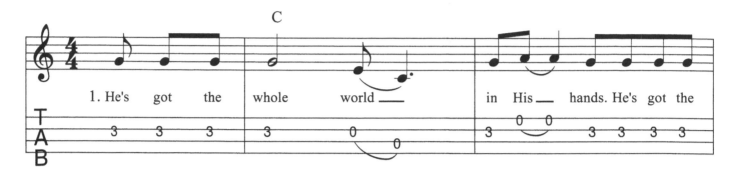

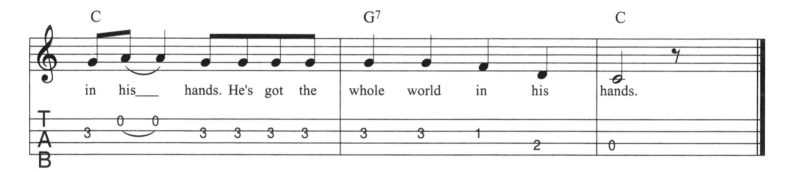

2. He's got you and me, sister, in His hands.

3. He's got you and me, brother, in His hands.

4. He's got the little tiny babies in His hands.

5. He's got the whole world in His hands.

1926 Music Magazine Advertisement

Pick A Bale Of Cotton

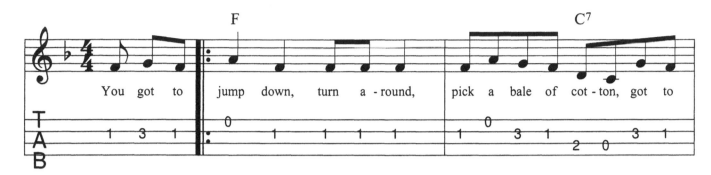

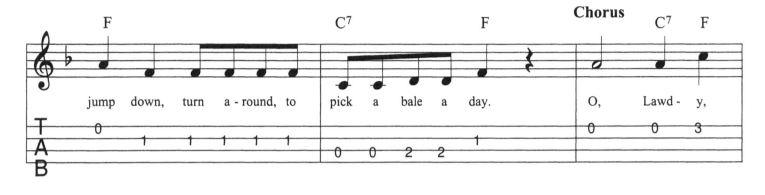

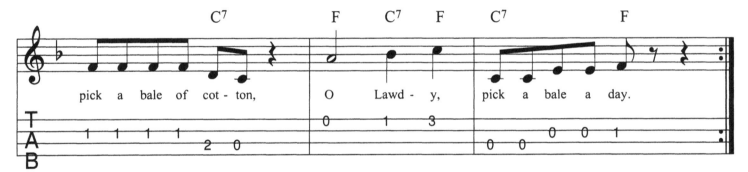

Me an' my partner can
Pick a bale of cotton,
Oh, me an' my partner can
Pick a bale a day.

Me an' my wife can
Pick a bale of cotton,
Oh, me an' my wife can
Pick a bale a day.

Had a little woman could
Pick a bale of cotton,
Oh, had a little woman could
Pick a bale a day.

I b'lieve to my soul I can
Pick a bale of cotton,
I b'lieve to my soul I can
Pick a bale a day.

Went to Corsicana to
Pick a bale of cotton,
Oh, went to Corsicana to
Pick a bale a day.

Rock Of Ages

Rock of a - ges, cleft for me, let me hide my -self in Thee, let the

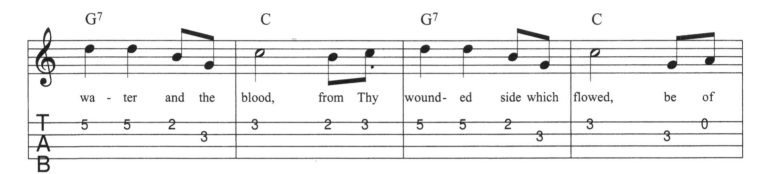

wa - ter and the blood, from Thy wound- ed side which flowed, be of

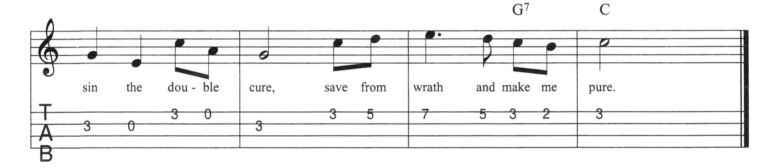

sin the dou - ble cure, save from wrath and make me pure.

Not the labours of my lands
 can fulfill the law's demands;
Could my zeal no respite know,
 could my tears for ever flow.
All for sin could not atone:
 thou must save, and thou alone.

Nothing in my hand I bring,
 simply to thy cross I cling.
Naked, come to thee for dress,
 helpless, look to thee for grace.
Foul, I to the fountain fly:
 wash me, Savior, or I die.

While I draw this fleeting breath,
 when my eyelids close in death.
When I soar to worlds unknown,
 see thee on thy judgment throne,
Rock of Ages, cleft for me,
 let me hide myself in thee.

Sweet Betsy From Pike

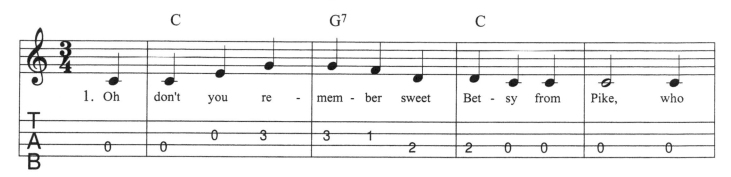

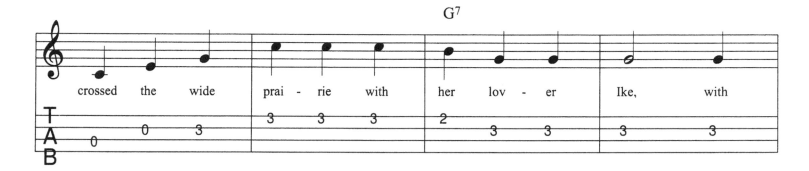

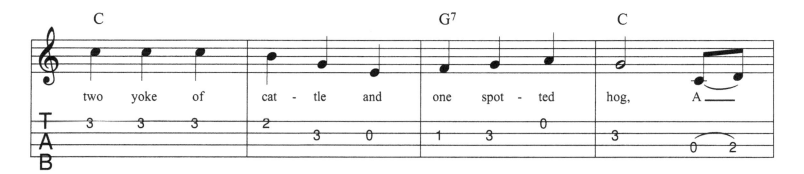

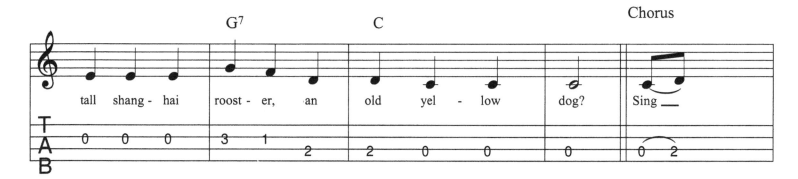

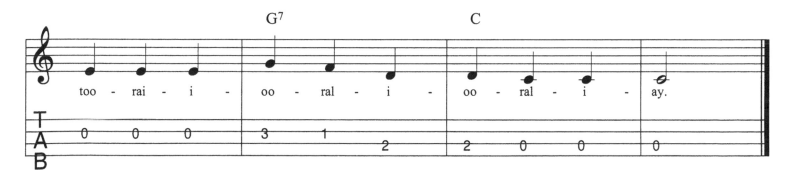

Songs With 3 Chords
Aloha Oe

Proud - ly swept the rain cloud by the cliff, as on it glid - ed through the

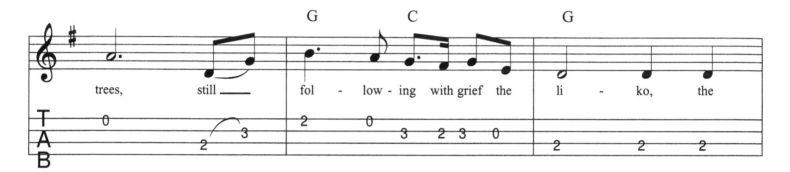

trees, still ____ fol - low - ing with grief the li - ko, the

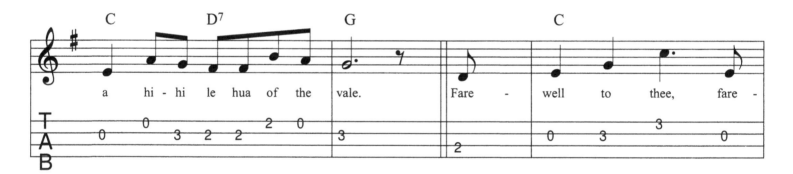

a hi - hi le hua of the vale. Fare - well to thee, fare -

well to thee, thou charm- ing one who dwells a -mong the bow- ers. One

fond em - brace be - fore I now de -part un - til we meet ____ a - gain.

Beautiful Kahana

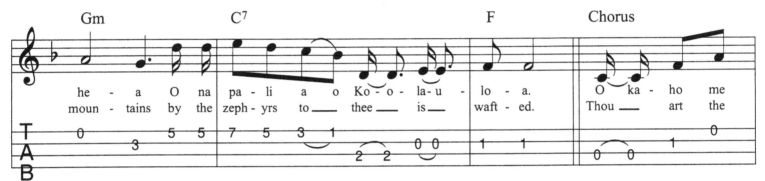

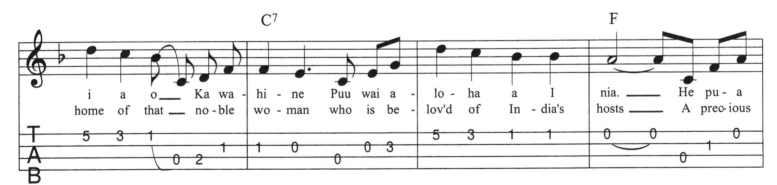

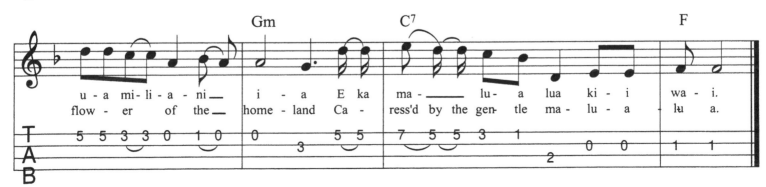

Camptown Races

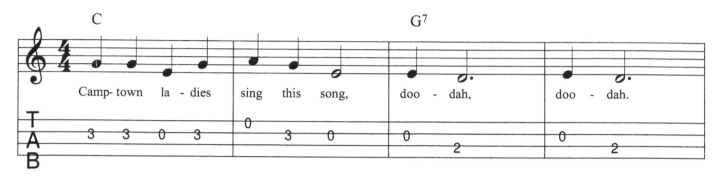

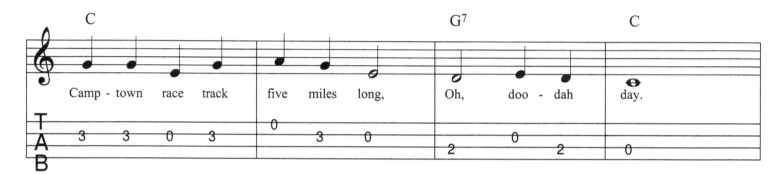

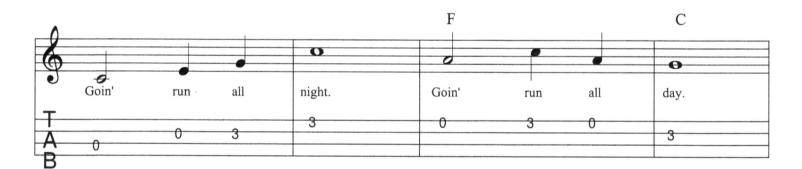

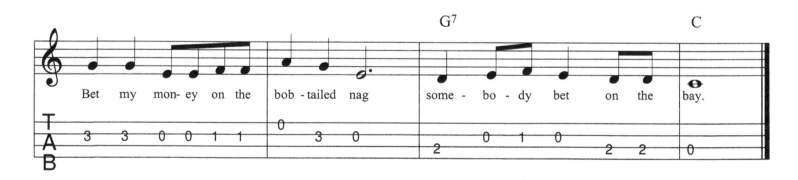

2. Went down there with my head caved in,
    Doo dah, doo dah,
    Came back home with a pocket full of tin,
    Oh, doo dah day.

Down By The Riverside

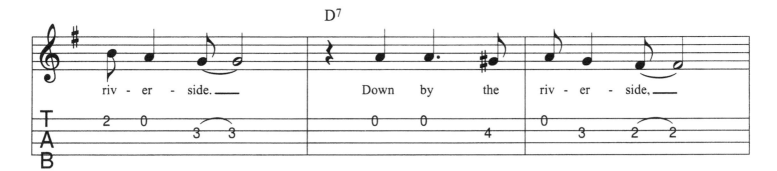

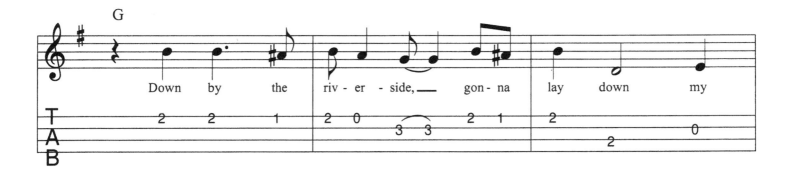

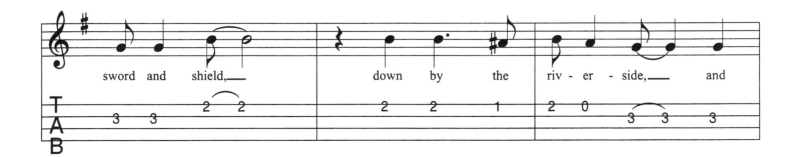

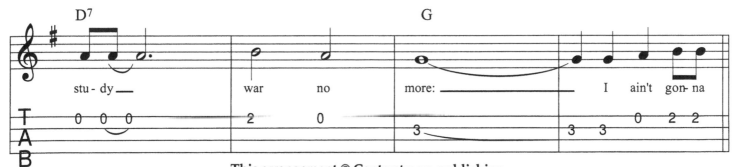

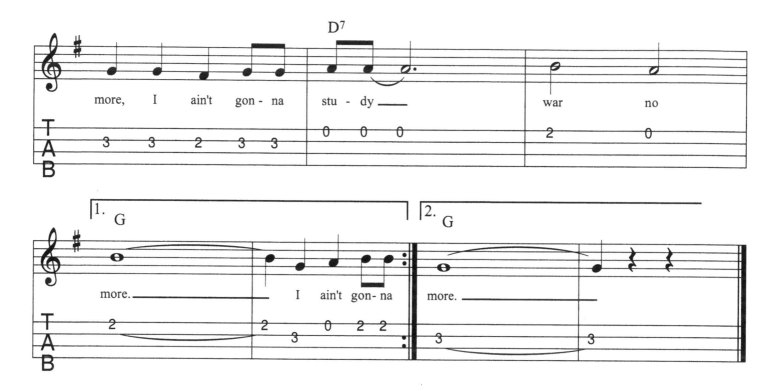

2. I'm gonna join hands with everyone, etc.

3. I'm gonna put on my long white robe, etc.

4. I'm gonna talk with the Prince of Peace, etc.

Early String Advertisement

Little Brown Jug

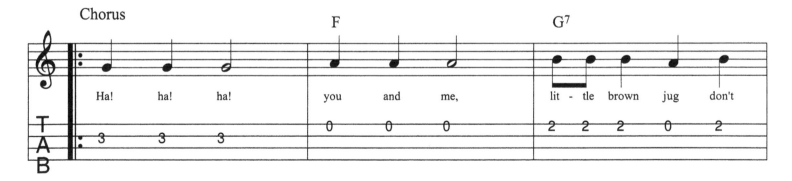

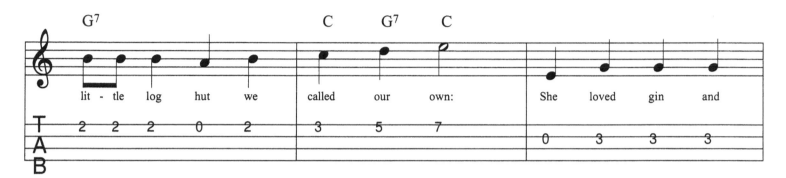

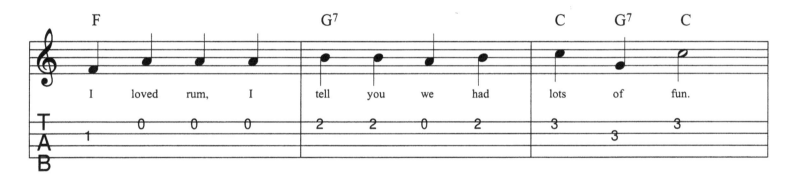

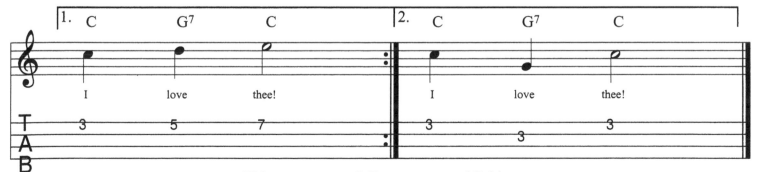

Maui Girl

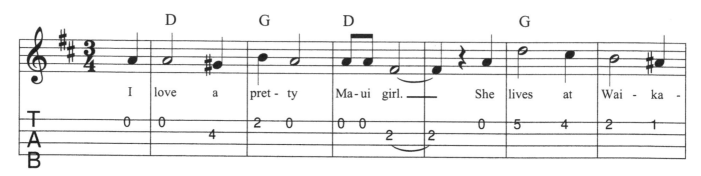

I love a pret-ty Ma-ui girl. ___ She lives at Wai-ka-

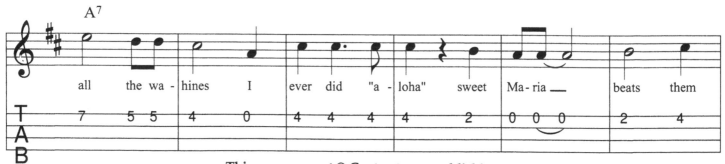

pu ___ with ros-y cheeks and pearl-y teeth ___ and

love-ly ___ nut brown hair ___ her waist is so

slen-der ___ and her o-pou so much nui-nui ___ and of

all the wa-hines I ever did "a-loha" sweet Ma-ria ___ beats them

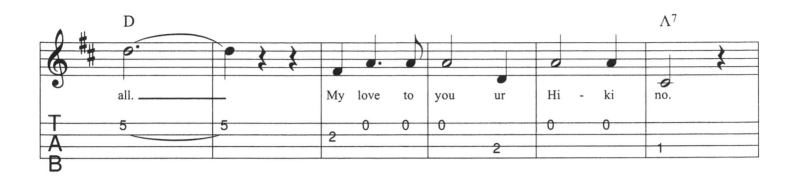

all. _____ My love to you ur Hi - ki no.

your love to me pe - la no Don't tell ma - ma ku-li-ku-li

she'll tell pa - pa lu-li-lu-li nui nui pili kia with me now. _____

Early Supertone Ukuleles Advertisement

Old MacDonald

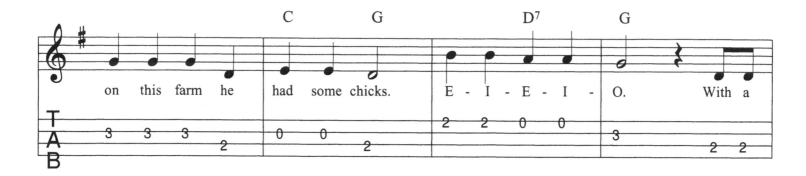

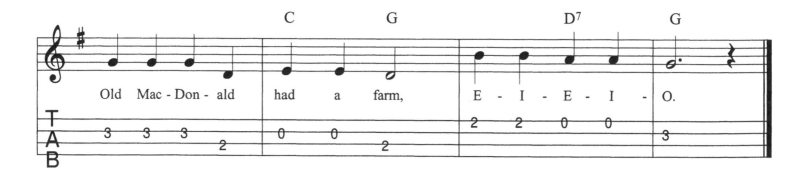

2. Ducks – Quack   5. Mules – Hee-haw

3. Turks – Gobble   6. Sheep – Baa-baa

4. Pigs – Oink

On Top Of Old Smoky

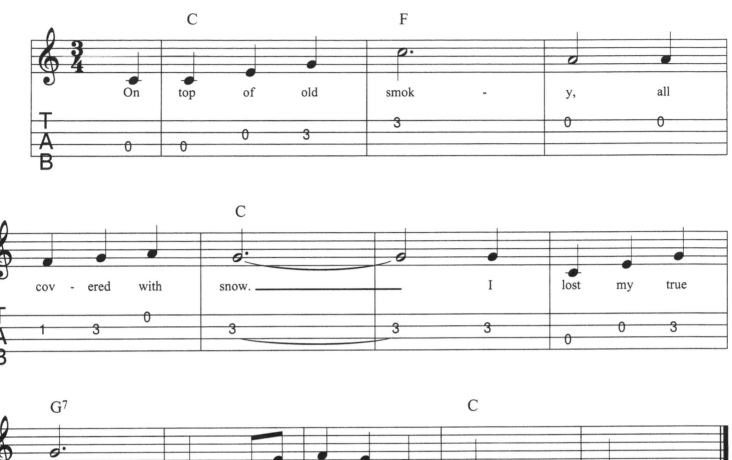

2. Oh courting's a pleasure and parting is grief
   But a false-hearted lover is worse than a thief.

3. A thief will not rob you of all that you have,
   But a false-hearted lover will lead to the grave.

4. The grave will decay you and turn you to dust,
   Not one in a million a poor girl can trust.

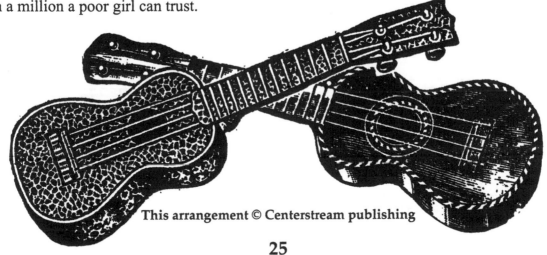

She'll Be Coming 'Round The Mountain

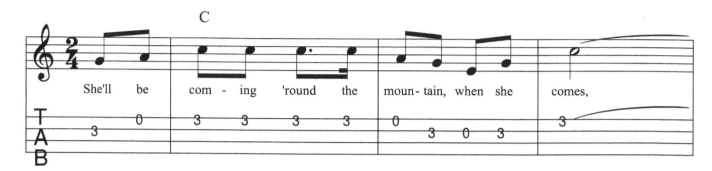

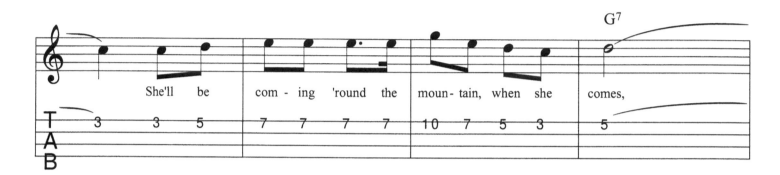

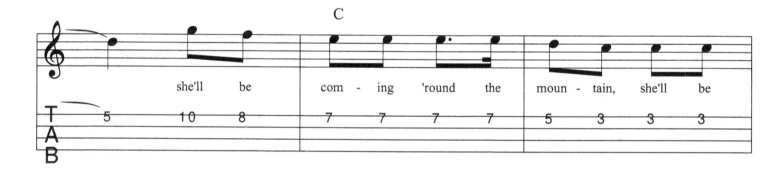

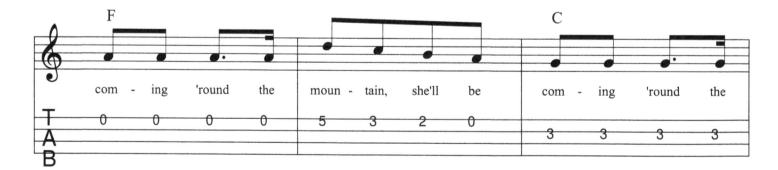

Silent Night

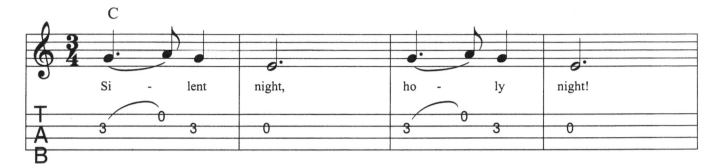

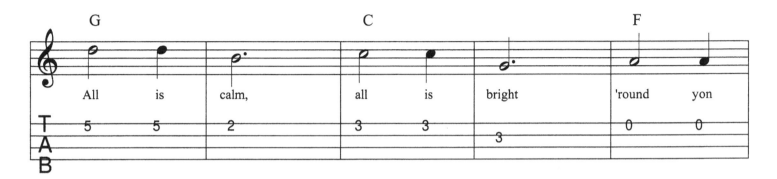

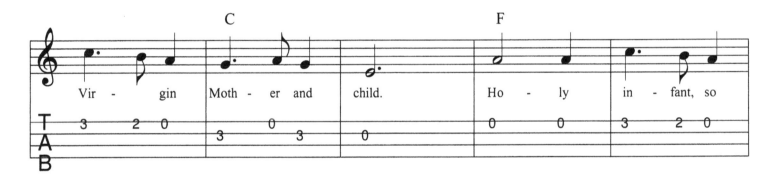

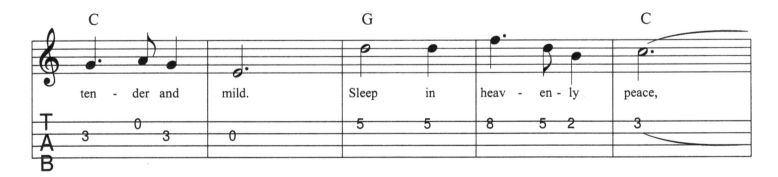

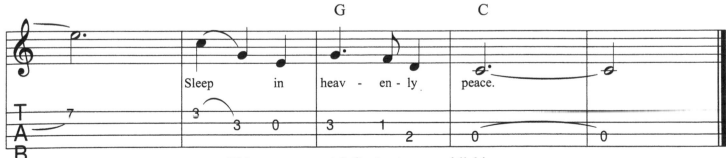

When The Saints Go Marchin' In

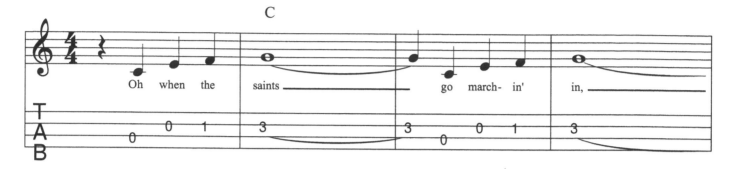

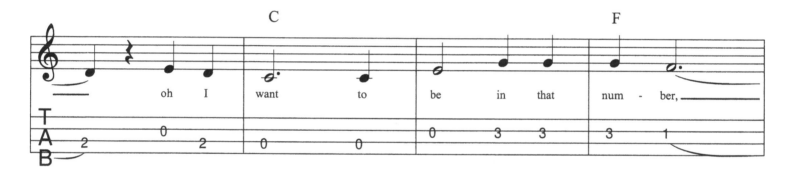

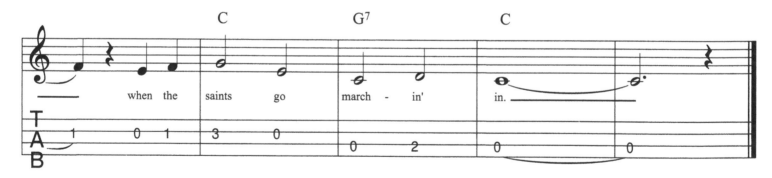

Oh, when the new world is revealed,
Oh, when the new world is revealed,
Oh Lord, I want to be in that number,
When the new world is revealed.

And when they crown Him Lord of all, (etc.)

And when the sun refuse to shine, (etc.)

Oh when they gather 'round the throne, (etc.)

Yellow Rose Of Texas

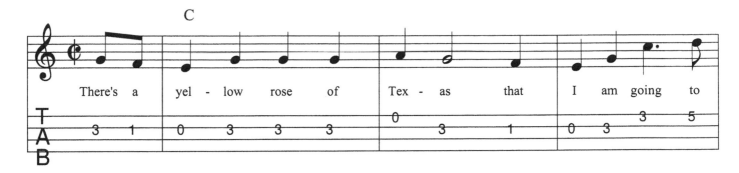

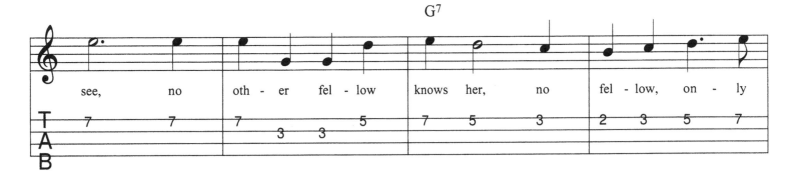

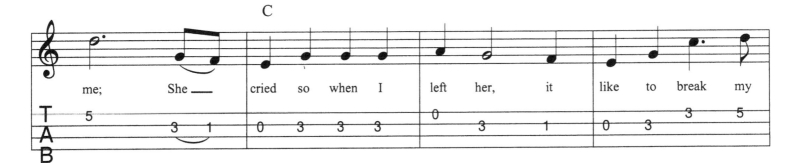

2. She's the sweetest rose of color
   a fellow ever knew,
   Her eyes are bright as di'monds
   they sparkle like the dew;
   You may talk about your dearest May
   and sing of Rosa Lee,
   But the Yellow Rose of Texas
   beats the belles of Tennessee.

3. Oh, now I'm going to find her,
   for my heart is full of woe,
   And we'll sing the song together,
   that we sung long ago;
   We'll play the banjo gaily,
   and we'll sing the songs of yore,
   And the Yellow Rose of Texas
   shall be mine forevermore.

This arrangement © Centerstream publishing

Songs With *4* Chords
Dixie

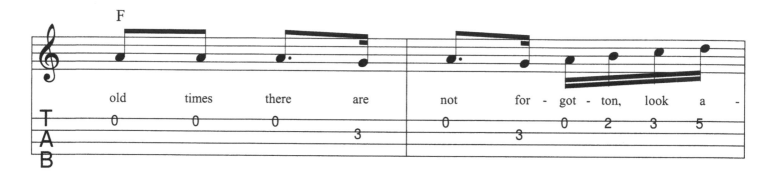

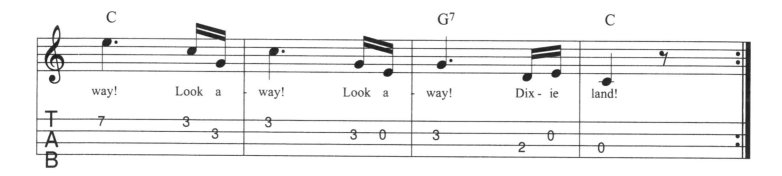

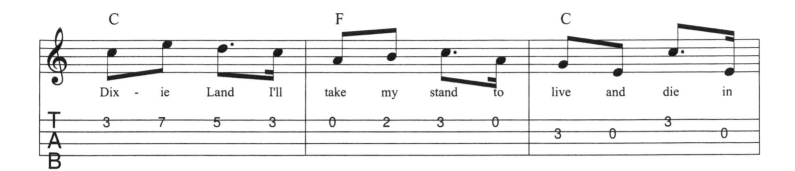

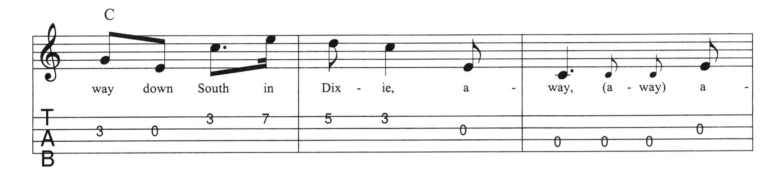

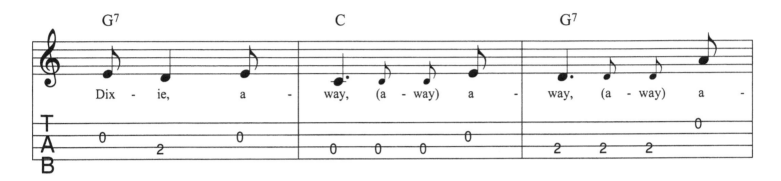

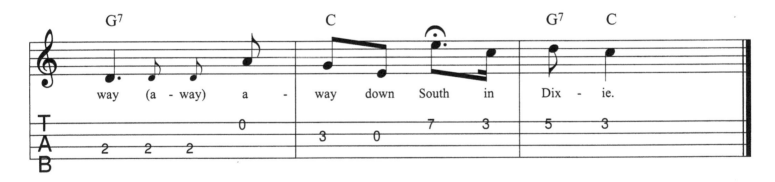

2. There's buckwheat cakes and indian batter, makes you fat or a little fatter,
Look away! Look away! Look away! Dixie Land!
Then hoe it down and scratch your gravel, to Dixie Land I'm bound to travel,
Look away! Look away! Look away! Dixie Land! *Chorus*

Oh, Susannah!

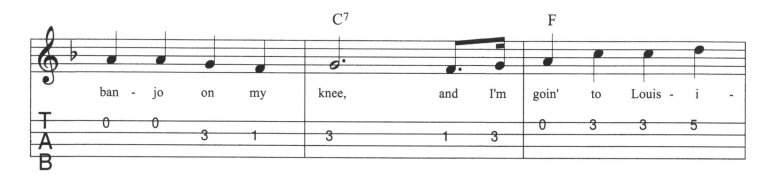

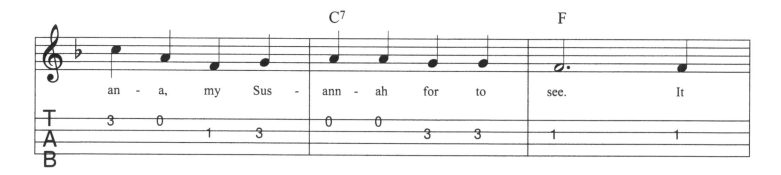

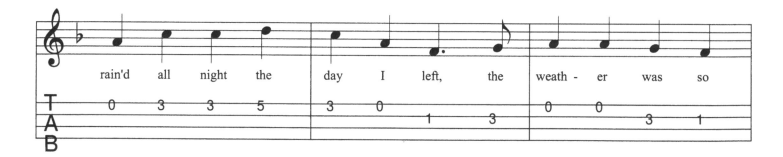

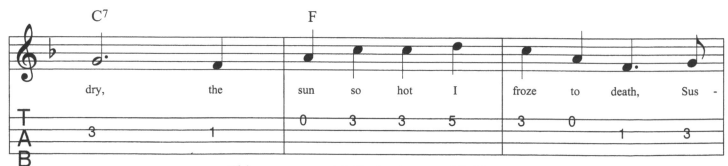

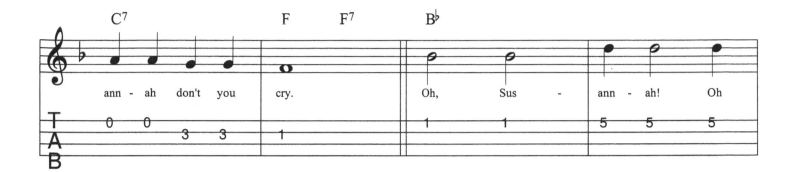

ann - ah don't you cry. Oh, Sus - ann - ah! Oh

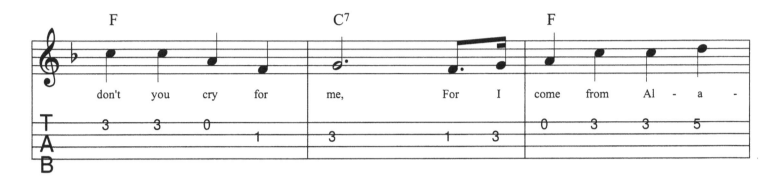

don't you cry for me, For I come from Al - a -

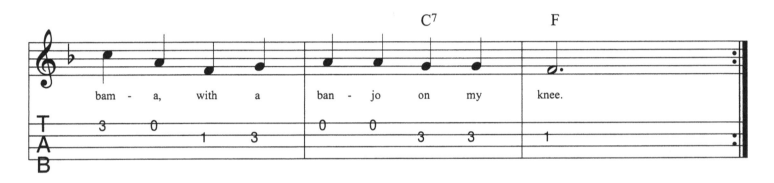

bam - a, with a ban - jo on my knee.

2. Oh, I had a dream the other nite when everything was still,
   And I thought I saw Susannah, just a comin' down the hill.
   A buckwheat cake was in her mouth, a tear was in her eye,
   I said I'm coming from the South, Susannah don't you cry. *Chorus*

Red River Valley

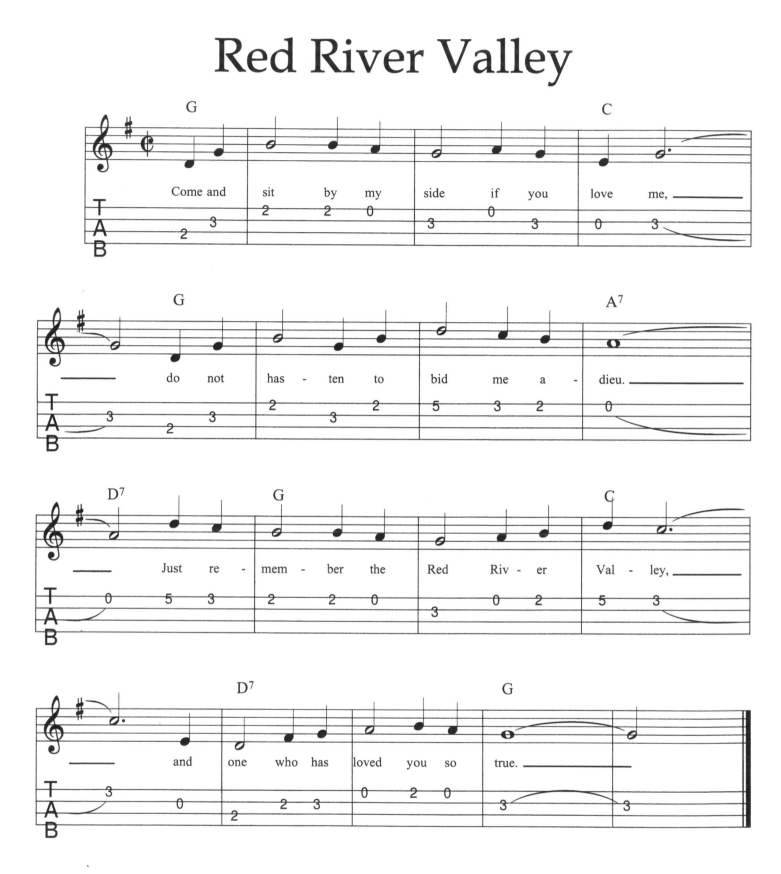

2. From this valley they say you are going,
   I will miss your sweet face and your smile
   Just because you are weary and tired,
   You are changing your range for awhile.
   Chorus

The Streets Of Laredo

Also known as "The Cowboy's Lament"

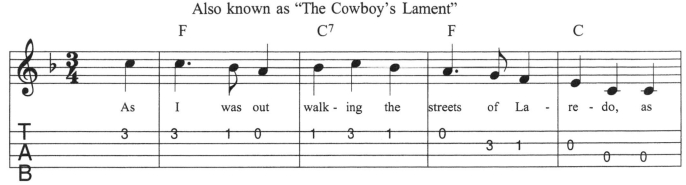

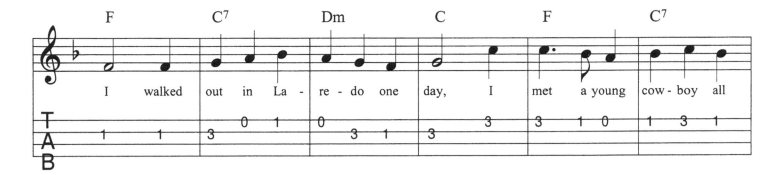

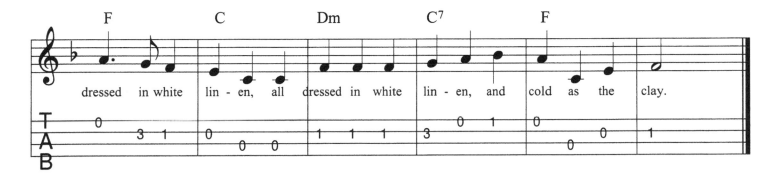

'O beat the drum slowly and play the fife lowly;
 play the Dead March as you carry me along.
Take me to the green valley and lay the sod o'er me,
 for I'm a young cowboy and I know I've done wrong.'

'I see by your outfit that you are a cowboy.'
 These words he did say as I boldly stepped by.
'Come sit down beside me and hear my sad story;
 I'm shot in the breast and I know I must die.'

'My friends and relations they live in the Nation;
 they know not where their dear boy has gone.
I first came to Texas and hired to a ranchman,
 O I'm a young cowboy and I know I've done wrong.'

'It was once in the saddle I used to go dashing;
 it was once in the saddle I used to go gay.
First to the dram house and then to the card house,
 got shot in the breast and I'm dying today.'

'Get six jolly cowboys to carry my coffin;
 get six pretty maidens to bear up my pall.
Put bunches of roses all over my coffin,
 put roses to deaden the clods as they fall.'

'Go gather around you a group of young cowboys,
 and tell them the story of this my sad fate.
Tell one and the other, before they go further,
 .to stop their wild roving before it's too late.'

'Go bring me a cup, a cup of cold water,
 to cool my parched lips, ' the young cowboy said.
Before I returned, the spirit had left him
 and gone to its Maker - the cowboy was dead.

We beat the drum slowed and played the fife lowly,
 and bitterly wept as we bore him along.
For we all loved our comrade, so brave, young and handsome,
 we all loved our comrade although he'd done wrong.

This arrangement © Centerstream publishing

Turkey In The Straw

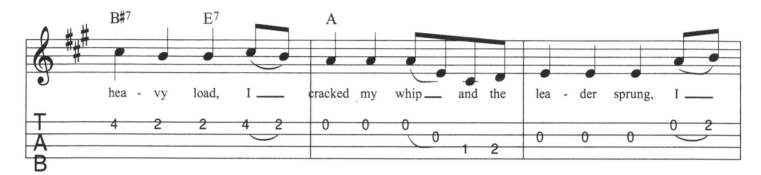

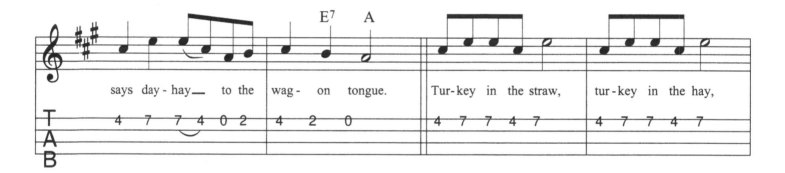

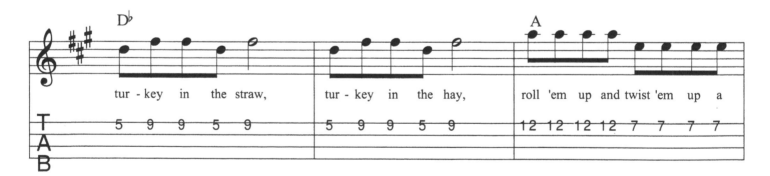

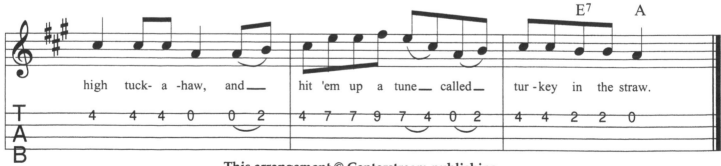

Yankee Doodle

This arrangement © Centerstream publishing

And there was Captain Washington
Upon a slapping stallion
A giving orders to his men;
I guess there were a million.

The flaming ribbons in his hat,
They look'd so tarnal fine, ah,
I wanted pockily to get
To give to my Jemimah.

And there they had a swampin' gun,
As big as a log of maple,
Upon a deuced little cart,
A load for father's cattle.

And every time they fired it off
It took a horn of powder;
It made a noise like father's gun,
Only a nation louder.

I went as nigh to it myself,
As 'Siah's underpinnin'.
And father went as near again –
I thought the deuce was in him.

And there I see a little keg;
Its heads were made of leather,
They knocked upon't with little sticks,
To call the folks together.

And there they'd fife away like fun,
And play on corn-stalk fiddles;
And some had ribbons red as blood,
All bound around their middles.

The troopers, too, would gallop up,
And fire right in our faces;
It scared me almost half to death,
To see them run such races.

Old Uncle Sam come there to change
Some pancakes and some onions
For 'lasses-cakes to carry home
To give his wife and young ones.

But I can't tell you half I see,
They kept up such a smother;
So I took my hat off, made a bow
And scampered home to mother.

Songs With *5* Chords
Amazing Grace

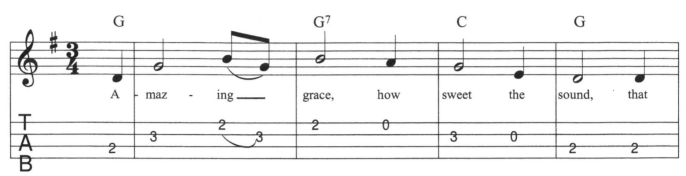

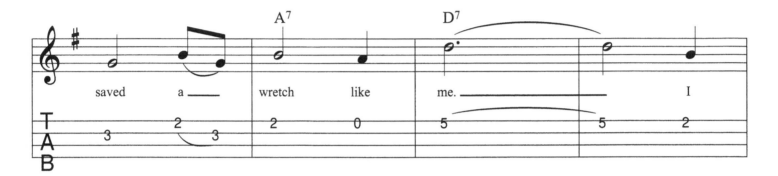

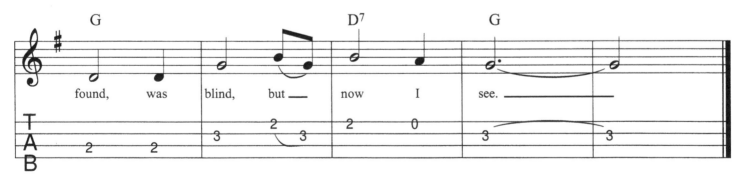

2. 'Twas grace that taught my heart to fear
   And grace my fears relieved;
   How precious did that grace appear
   The hour I first believed!

3. Thro' many dangers, toils and snares,
   I have already come;
   'Tis grace hath bro't me safe thus far,
   And grace will lead me home.

4. When we've been there ten thousand years,
   Bright shining as the sun,
   We've no less days to sing God's praise
   Than when we first begun.

Careless Love

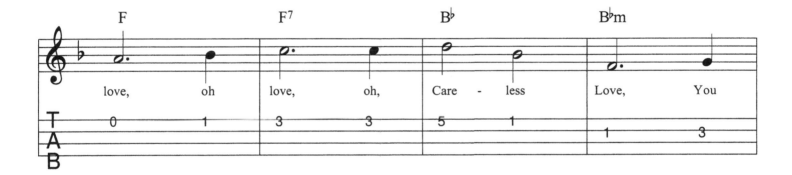

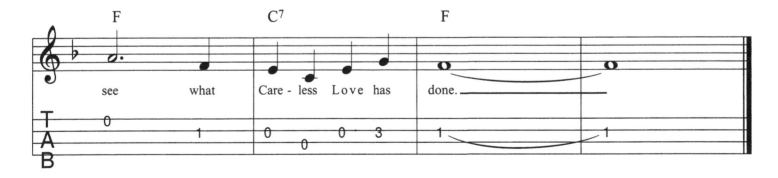

Goodbye, Ol' Paint

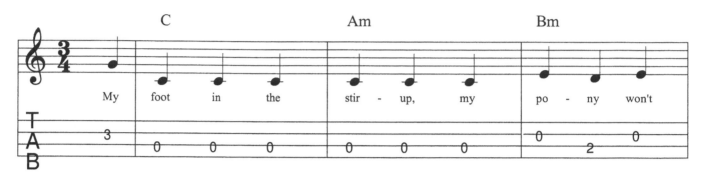

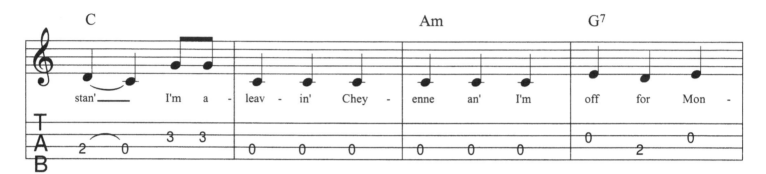

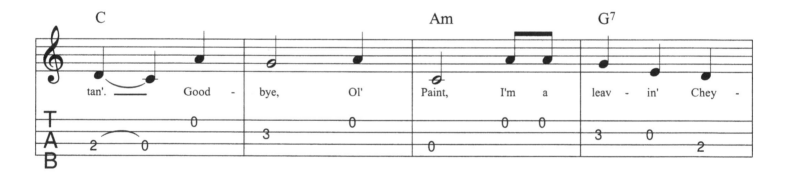

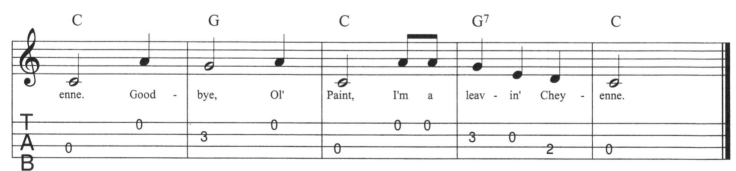

I'm riding Old Paint, I'm leading Old Dan,
I'm off for Cheyenne to do the hoolihan.
My foot's in the stirrup, my pony won't stand:

Old Paint's a good pony, he paces when he can,
Good-bye, my little Annie, I'm off for Cheyenne.

Go hitch up your horses and feed 'em some hay,
And sit yourself by me as long as you'll stay.

My horses ain't hungry, they won't eat your hay,
My wagon is loaded and rolling away.

They feed in the doulies, they water in the draw,
Their tails are all matted, their backs are all raw.

Bill Jones had two daughters and a song,
One went to Denver, the other went wrong.

His wife she died in a barroom fight,
And still he sings from morning till night.

Oh, when I die, take my saddle from the wall,
Put it on my pony and lead him from the stall;

Tie my bones to his back, turn our faces to the West
And we'll ride the prairie that we have loved best.

Haole Hula

R. A. Anderson

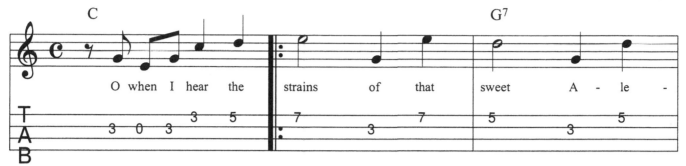

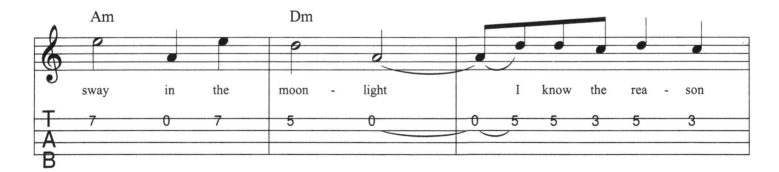

Home On The Range

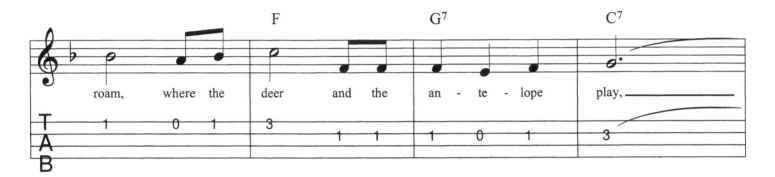

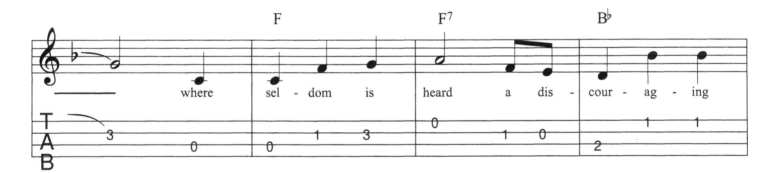

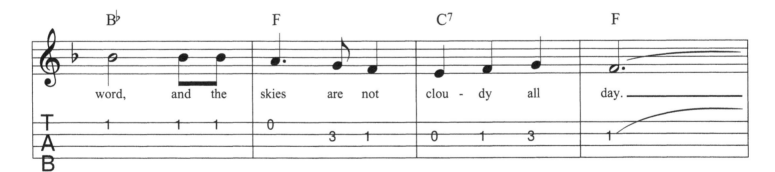

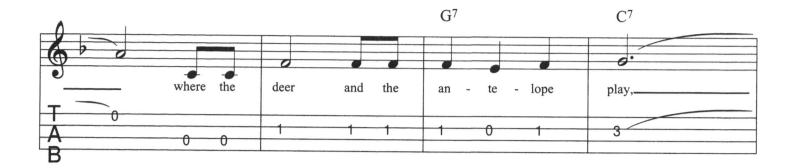

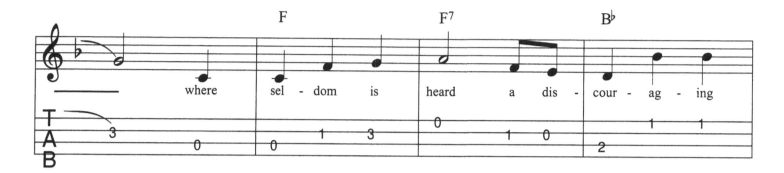

where the deer and the an - te - lope play,

where sel - dom is heard a dis - cour - ag - ing

word, and the skies are not clou - dy all day.

Oh, give me a land, where the bright diamond sand
 flows leisurely down the stream;
Where the graceful white swan, goes gliding along
 like a maid in a heavenly dream.

Oh, air is so pure, the zephyrs so free,
 the breezes so balmy and bright.
That I would not exchange my home on the range
 for all of the cities so bright.

Oh, often at night, when the heavens are bright
 with the light of the glittering stars.
Have I stood there amazed, and asked as I gazed
 if their glory exceeds that of ours.

Songs With 6 Chords
Abide With Me

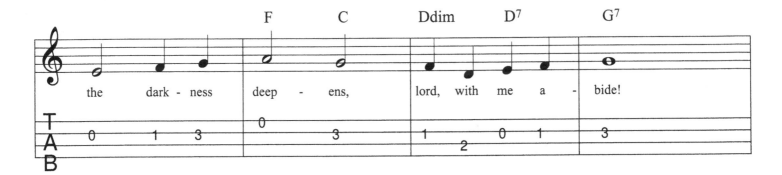

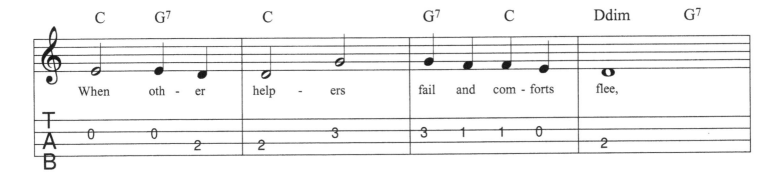

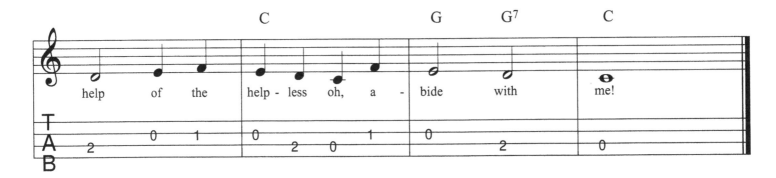

Swift to its close ebbs out life's little day;
 earth's joys go dim, its glories pass away.
Change and decay in all around I see:
O thou who changest not, abide with me!

I need thy presence every passing hour;
 what but thy grace can foil the tempter's power?
Who like thyself my guide and stay can be?
 Through cloud and sunshine, oh, abide with me.

I fear no foe, with thee at hand to bless;
 ills have no weight, and tears no bitterness.
Where is death's sting? Where, grave, thy victory?
 I triumph still if thou abide with me.

Hold thou thy cross before my closing eyes,
 shine through the gloom, and point me to the skies;
Heaven's morning breaks, and earth's vain shadows flee:
 in life, in death, O Lord, abide with me!

Deck The Halls

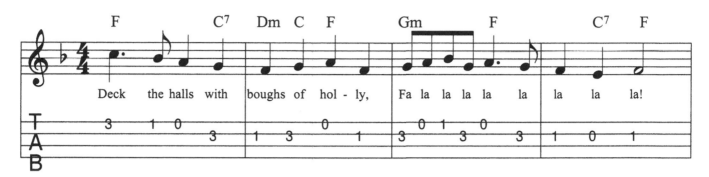

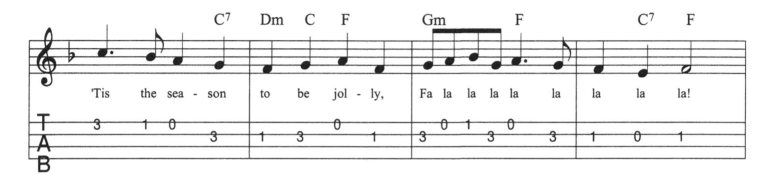

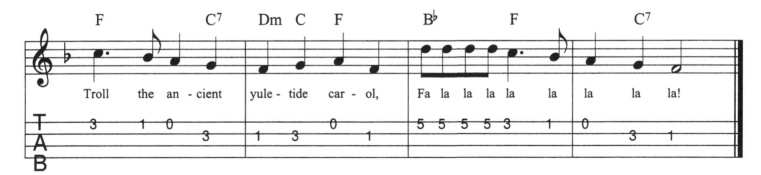

See the blazing yule before us,
Fa la la la la la la la la!
Strike the harp and join the chorus,
Fa la la la la la la la la!
Follow me in merry measure,
Fa la la la la la la la la!
While I tell of yule tide treasure.
Fa la la la la la la la la!

Fast away the old year passes
Fa la la la la la la la la!
Hail the new, ye lads and lasses,
Fa la la la la la la la la!
Sing we joyous all together,
Fa la la la la la la la la!
Heedless of the wind and weather.
Fa la la la la la la la la!

Ida

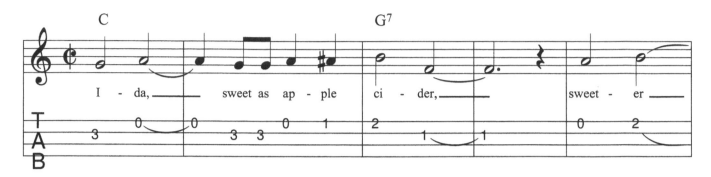

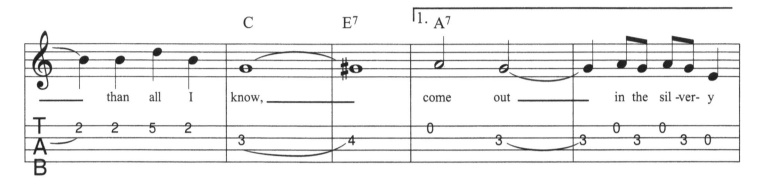

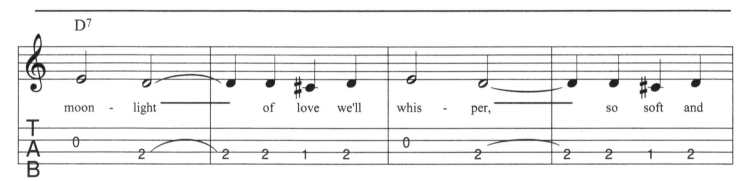

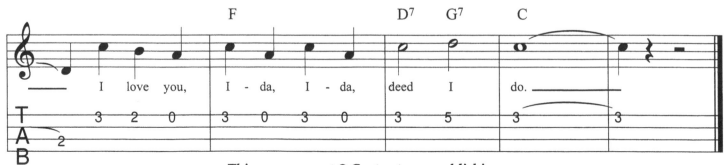

Jingle Bells

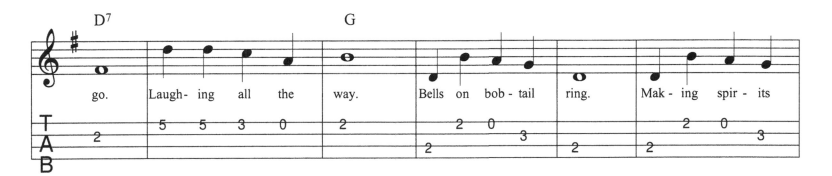

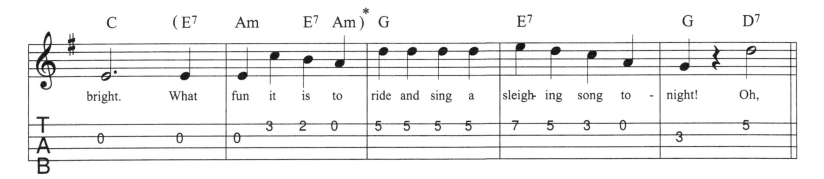

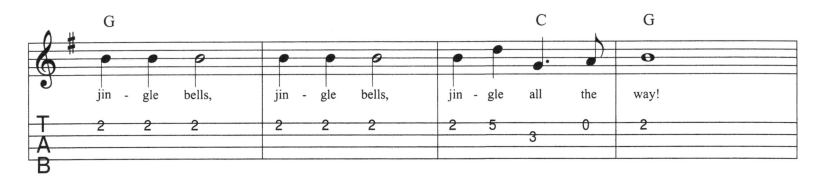

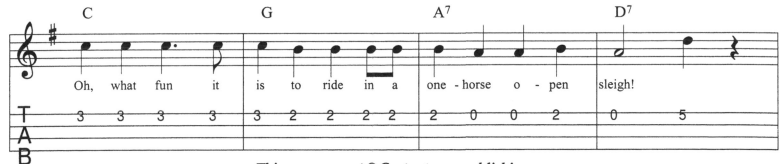

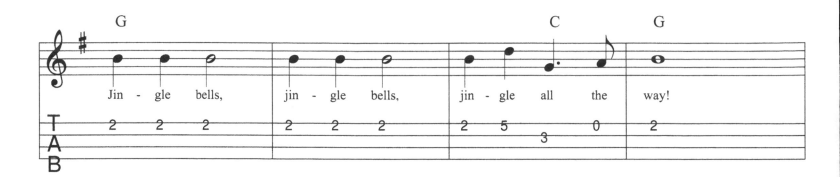

Jin - gle bells,   jin - gle bells,   jin - gle all the way!

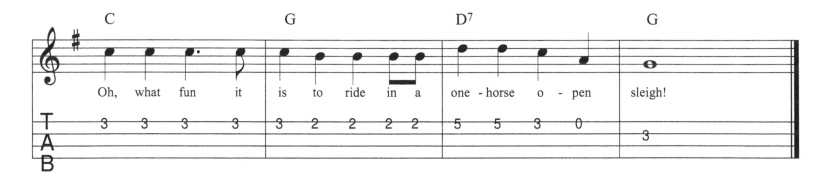

Oh, what fun it is to ride in a one - horse o - pen sleigh!

William Bill Tapia

48

May Day Is Lei Day In Hawaii

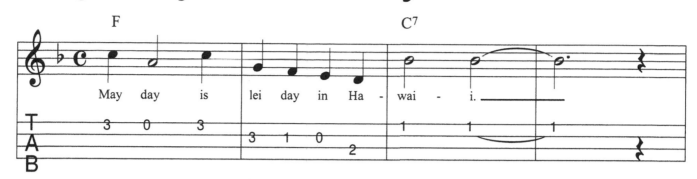

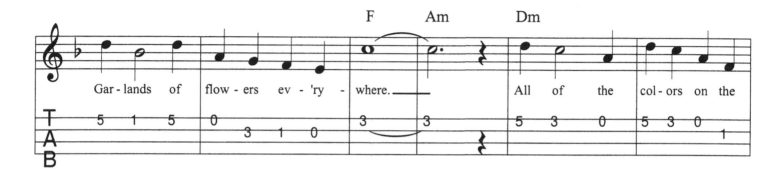

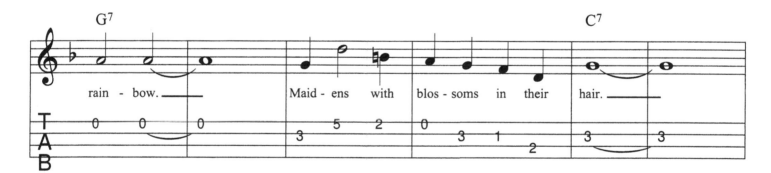

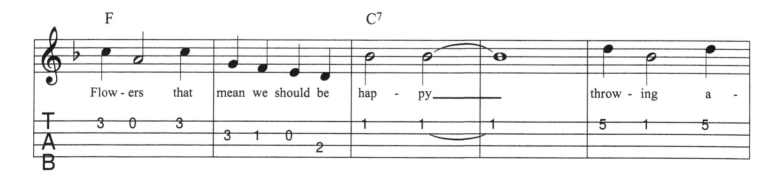

wa - i - i   Lei Day is hap-py day out there.

© Centerbrook

Na Lei O Hawaii

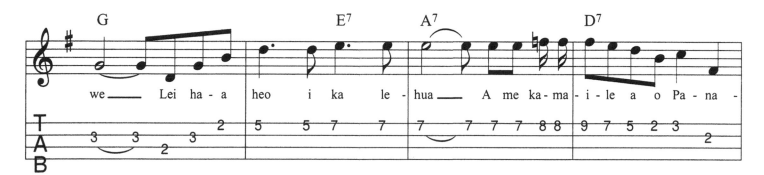

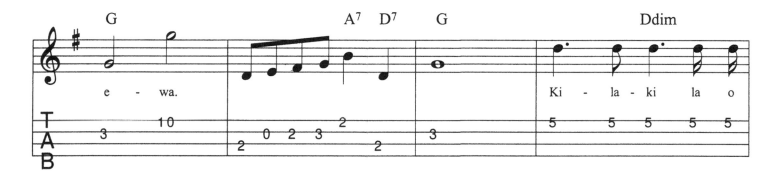

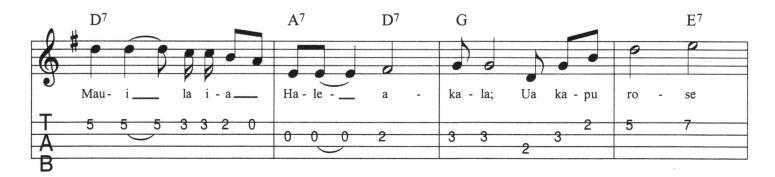

Shenandoah

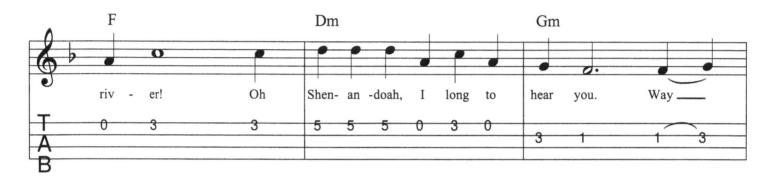

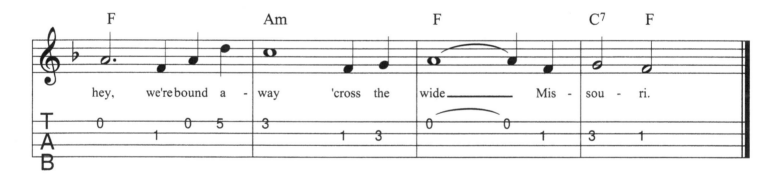

Strawberry Roan

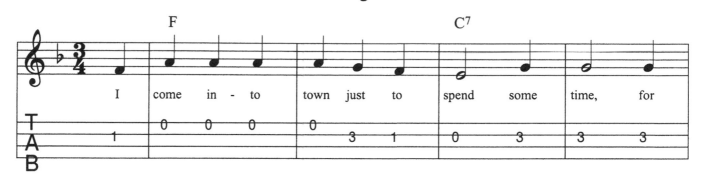

I come in - to town just to spend some time, for

I had no mon - ey, not e - ven a dime. Then a

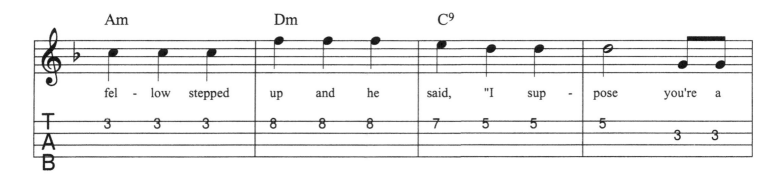

fel - low stepped up and he said, "I sup - pose you're a

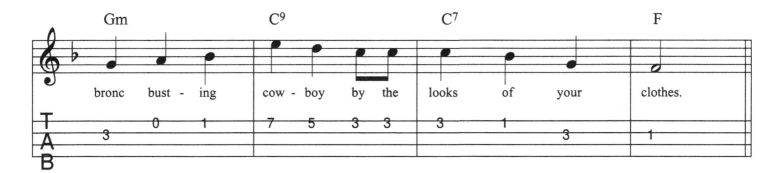

bronc bust - ing cow - boy by the looks of your clothes.

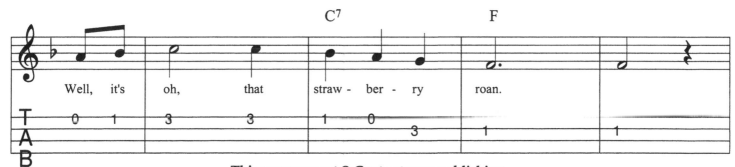

Well, it's oh, that straw - ber - ry roan.

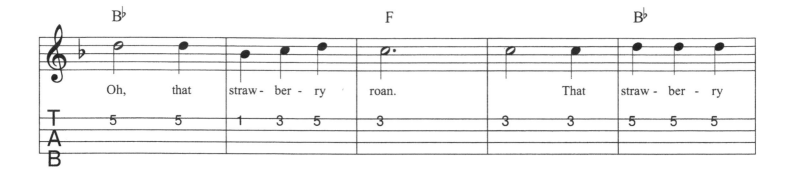

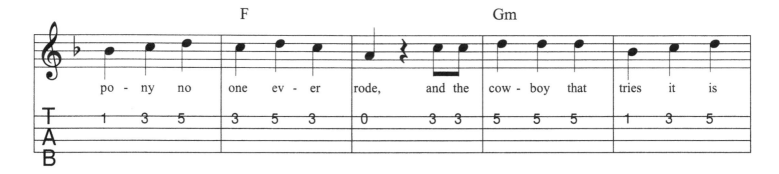

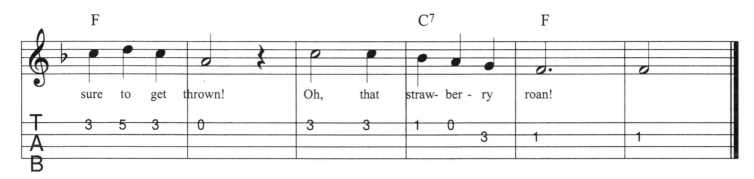

2. I gits all excited and asks what he pays
To ride that old horse for a couple of days.
He offers me ten, and I says, 'I'm your man,
'Cause the horse hasn't lived that I couldn't fan.
He says, 'Git your saddle, and I'll give you a chance,'
So we climb in the buckboard and ride to the ranch.
Early next morning right after chuck
I go down to see if this outlaw can buck.

3. There in the corral just a-standing alone
Is a scrawny old pony – a strawberry roan.
He has little pig eyes and a big Roman nose,
Long spavined legs that turn in at the toes,
Little pin ears that are split at the tip,
And a 44 brand there upon his left hip.
I put on my spurs and I coil up my twine,
And say to the stranger, 'That ten-spot is mine.'

4. Then I put on the blinds and it sure is a fight.
My saddle comes next, and I screw it down tight.
Then I pile on his back and well I know then,
If I ride this old pony, I'll sure earn my ten.
For he bows his old neck and he leaps from the ground
Ten circles he makes before coming down.
He's the worse bucking bronc I've seen on the range,
He can turn on a nickel and give you some change.

5. He goes up again and he turns round and round.
As if he's quit living down there on the ground.
He turns his old belly right up to the sun;
He sure is a sunfishing son-of-a-gun.
He goes up in the East and comes down in the West,
To stay in the saddle, I'm doin' my best.
I lose both my stirrups and also my hat,
And start pullin' leather as blind as a bat.

6. He goes up once more, and he goes way up high,
And leaves me a-settin' up there in the sky.
I turn over twice and I come down to earth,
And I start into cussin' the day of his birth.
I've rode lots of ponies out here on the range,
And there's been one or two that I shore couldn't tame.
But I'll bet all my money there's no man alive
Can ride that old horse when he makes his high dive.

Songs With 7 or More Chords
Bill Bailey

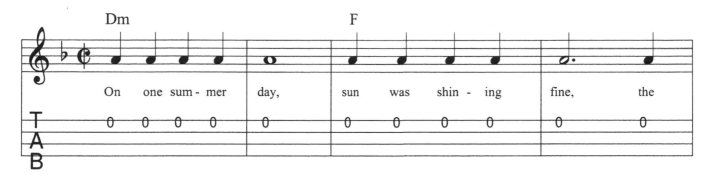

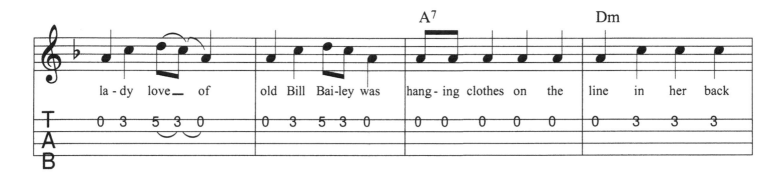

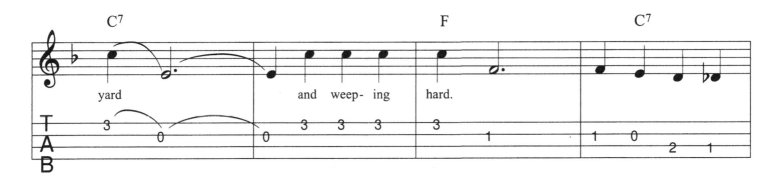

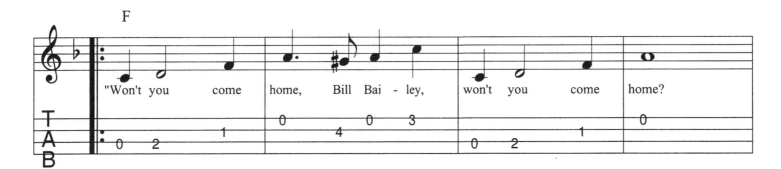

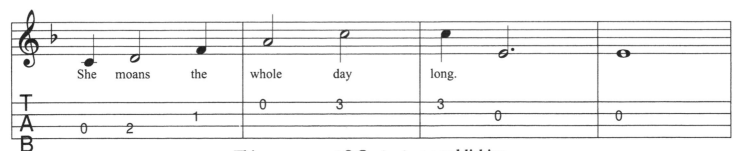

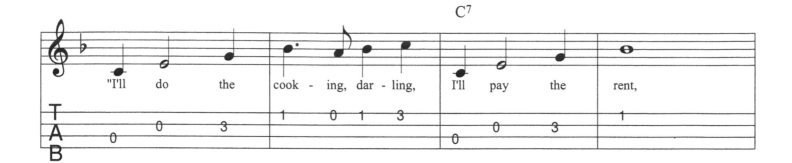

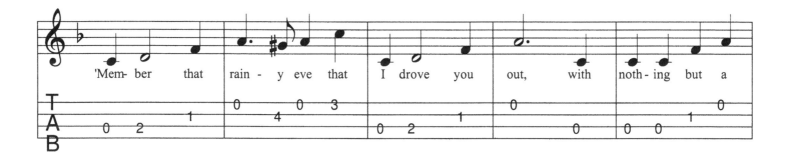

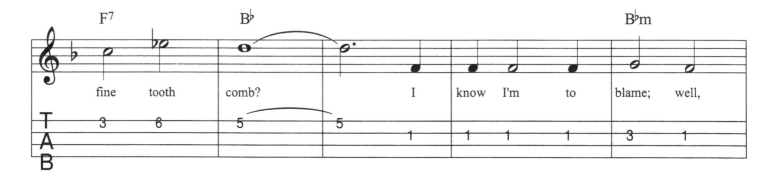

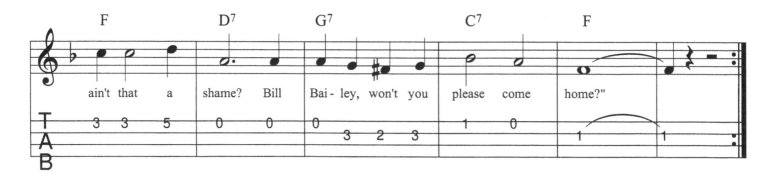

Hawaii, Moonlight, Flowers and You

Paul Summers

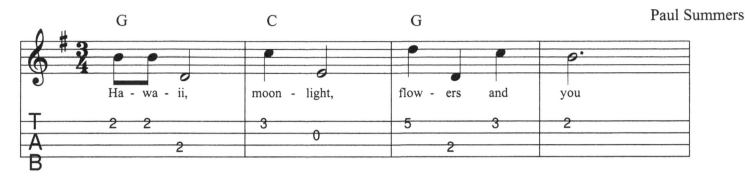

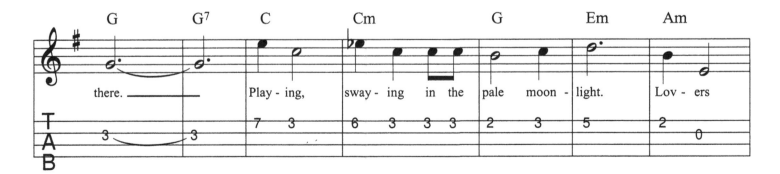

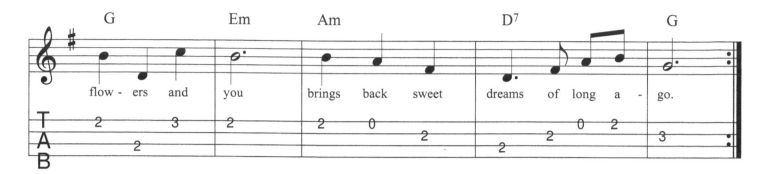

flow - ers and you brings back sweet dreams of long a - go.

Holy, Holy, Holy

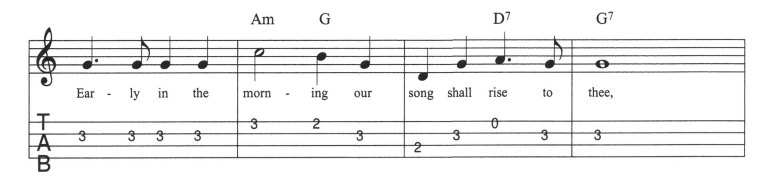

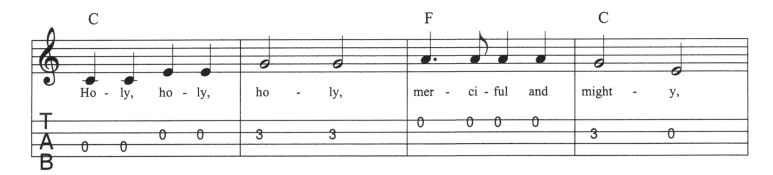

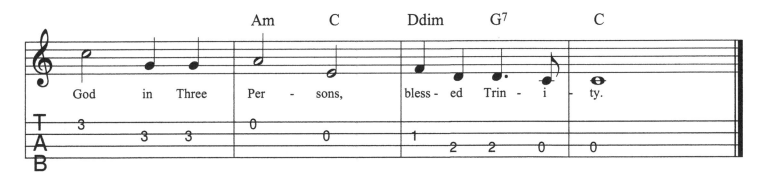

Holy, holy, holy; all the saints adore thee,
Casting down their golden crowns around the glassy sea;
Cherubim and seraphim falling down before thee,
Who wert, and art, and evermore shalt be.

Holy, holy, holy, Lord God Almighty!
All thy works shall praise thy name in earth and sky and sea;
Holy, holy, holy, merciful and mighty,
God in three Persons, blessed Trinity!

In The Good Old Summertime

In the good old sum - mer time, _____ In the

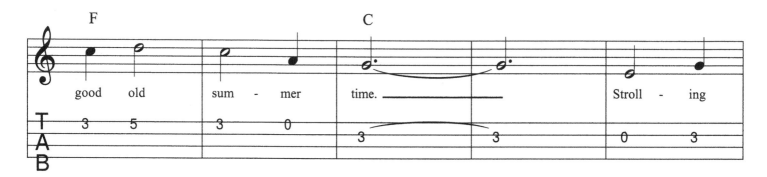

good old sum - mer time. _____ Stroll - ing

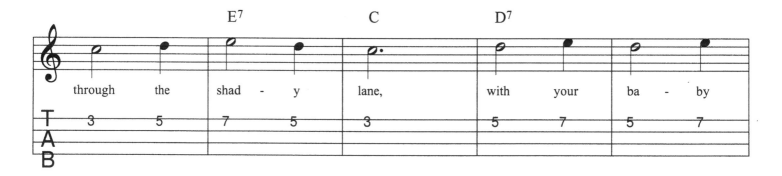

through the shad - y lane, with your ba - by

mine. _____ You hold her hand and she holds

yours, and that's a ve - ry good sign, _____ that

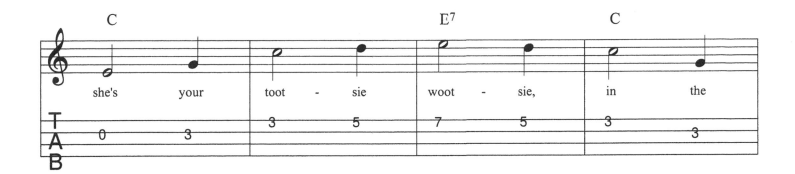

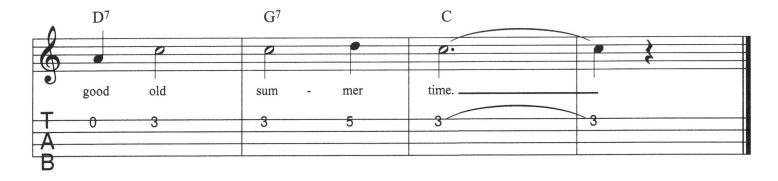

Melody Of Love

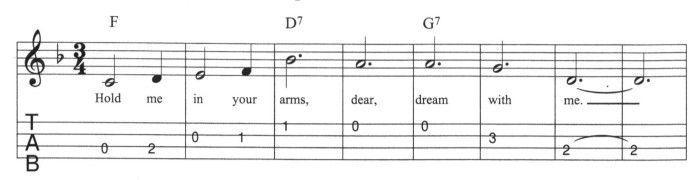

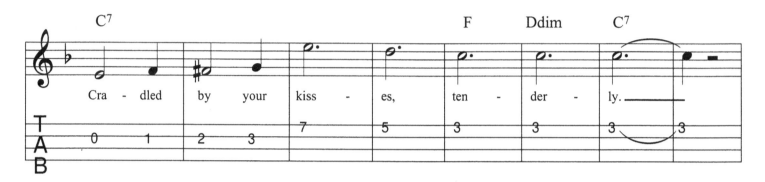

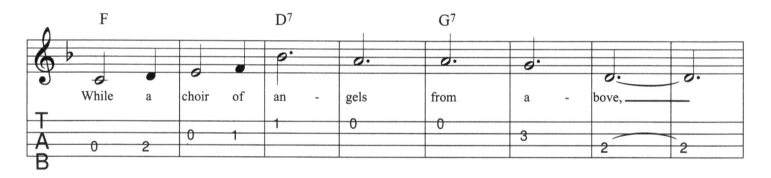

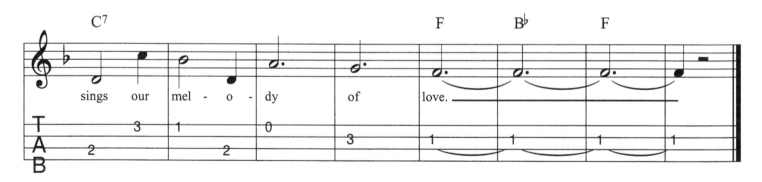

This arrangement © Centerstream publishing

My Wild Irish Rose

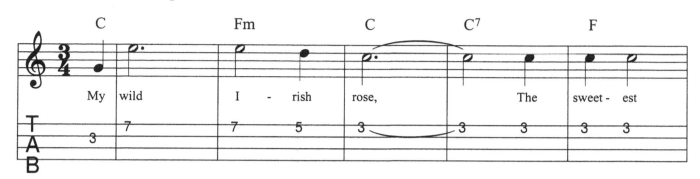

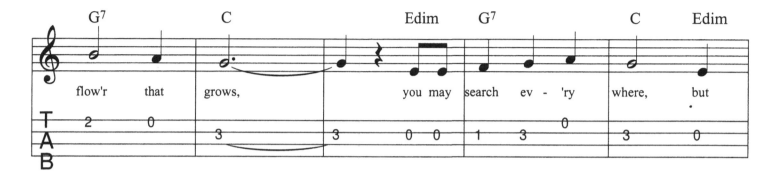

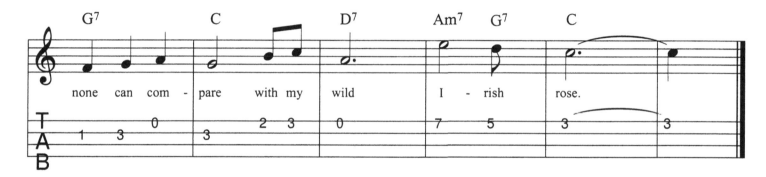

If you listen, I'll sing you a sweet little song
Of a flower that's now drooped and dead.
Yet dearer to me, yes, than all of its mates
Though each holds aloft its proud head.

'Twas given to me by a girl that I know,
Since we've met, faith, I've known no repose.
She is dearer by far, than the world's brightest star
And I call her my wild Irish rose.

My wild Irish rose, the dearest flower that grows,
And some day for my sake, she may let me take
The bloom from my wild Irish rose.

O Little Town Of Bethlehem

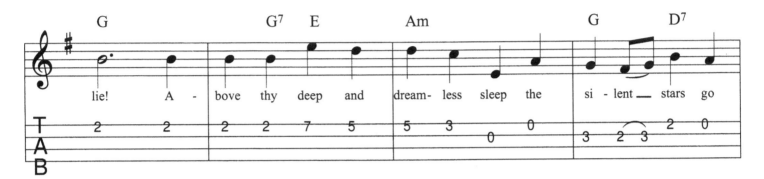

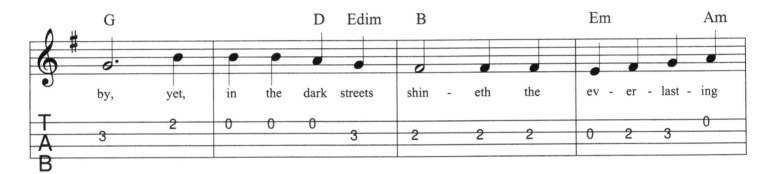

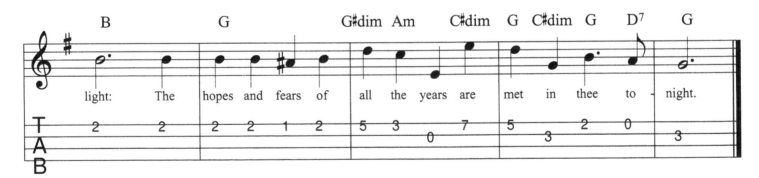

2. How silently, how silently,
   The wondrous gift is given!
   So God imparts to human hearts,
   The blessings of His heav'n,
   No ear may hear His coming,
   But in this world of sin
   Where meek souls will receive Him still,
   The dear Christ enters in.

3. O holy Child of Bethlehem,
   Descend to us we pray;
   Cast out our sin and enter in,
   Be born in us today,
   We hear the Christmas angels
   The great glad tiding tell;
   O come to us, abide with us,
   Our Lord Emmanuel.

Sweet Rosie O'Grady

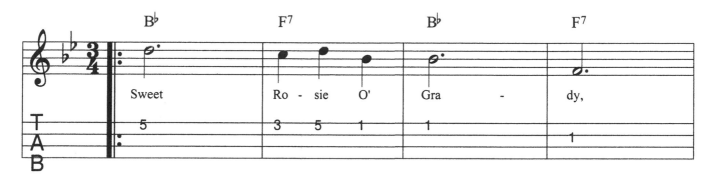

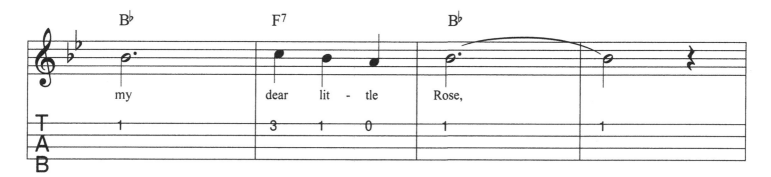

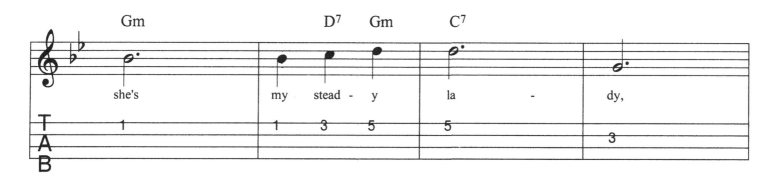

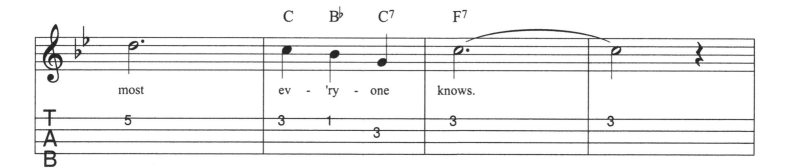

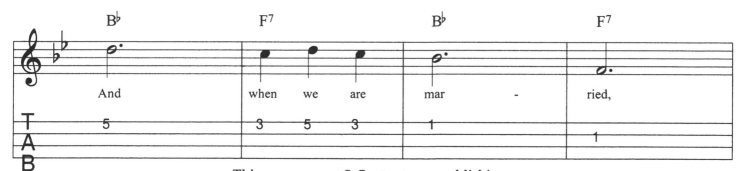

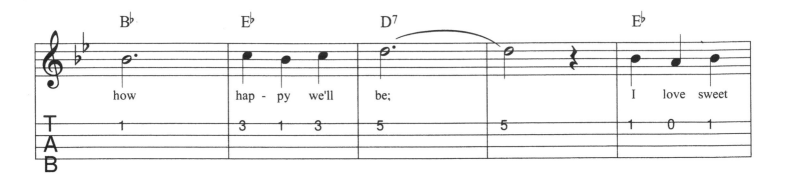

how   hap - py we'll   be;   I love sweet

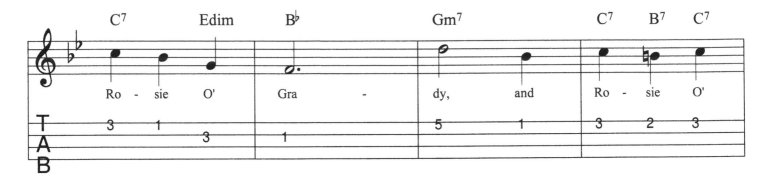

Ro - sie O'   Gra -   dy,   and   Ro - sie O'

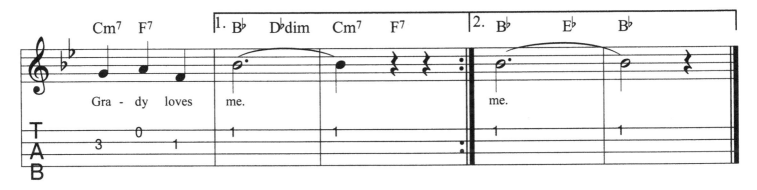

Gra - dy loves   me.   me.

That's What The Lei Said To Me

(<u>Lei</u> pronounced 'lay') Hawaiian for wreath of flowers

words and music by
Alfred Perez

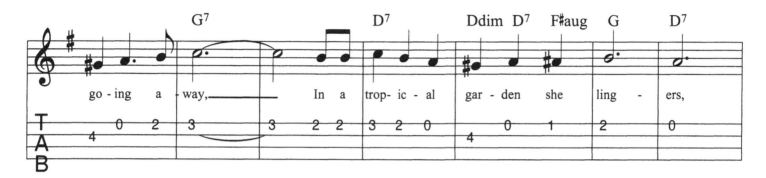

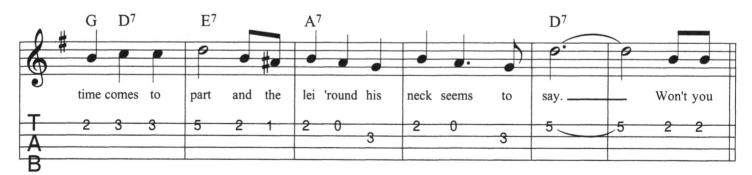

Chorus

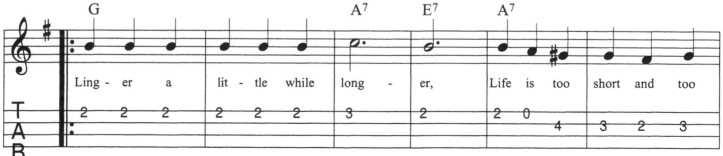

This arrangement © Centerstream publishing

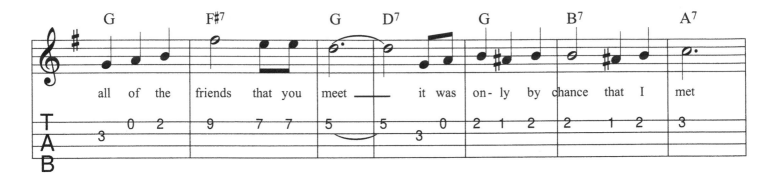

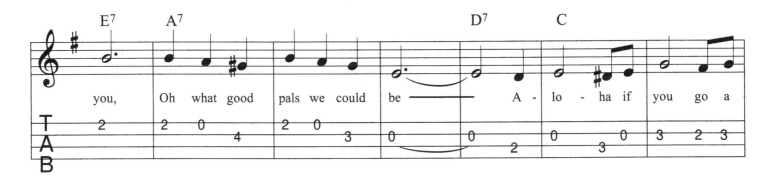

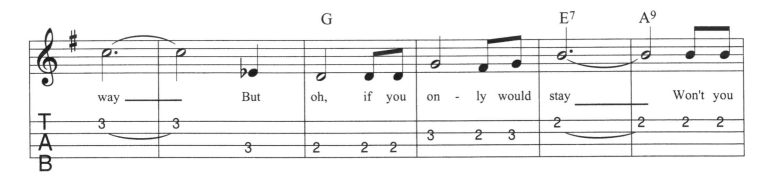

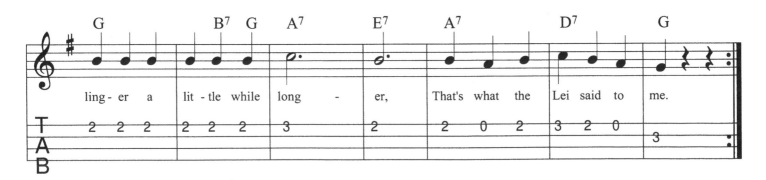

Under Aloha Moon

Paul Summers

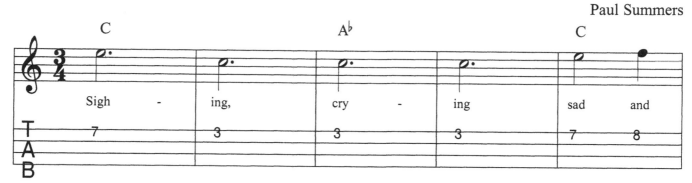

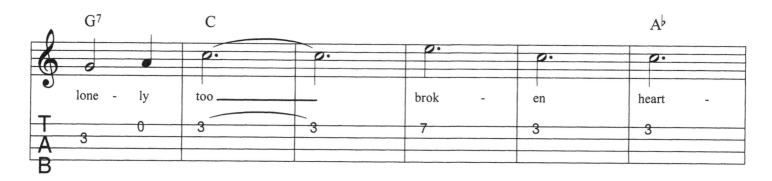

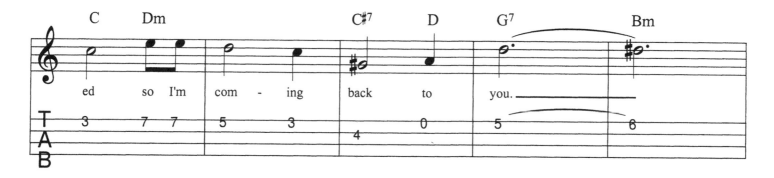

Chorus

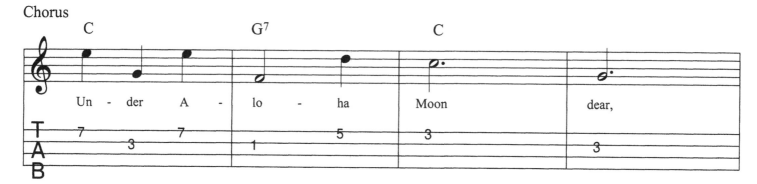

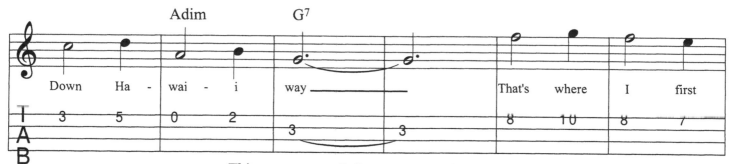

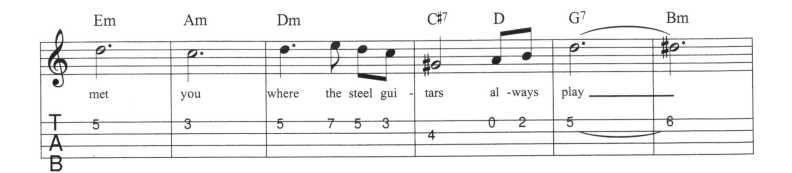

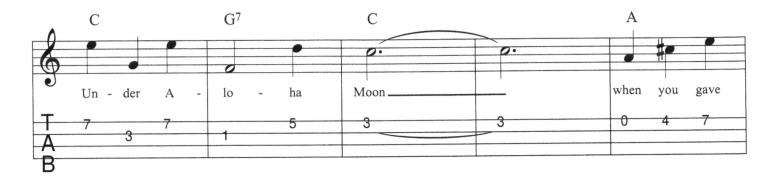

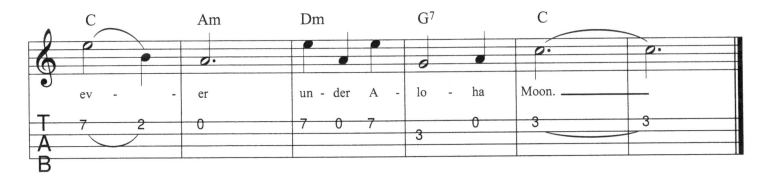

What Aloha Means

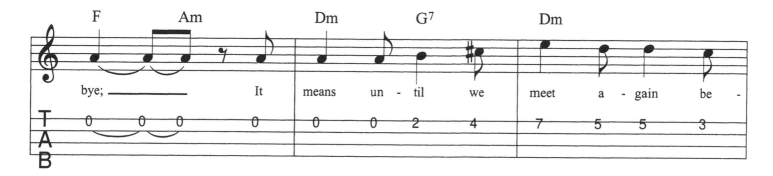

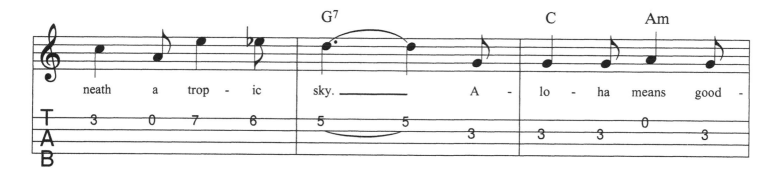

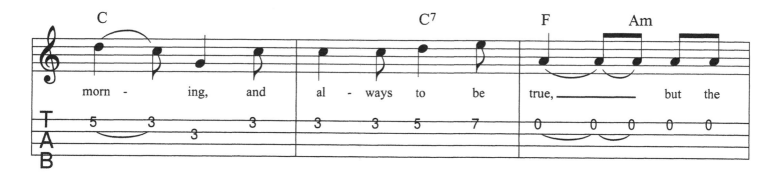

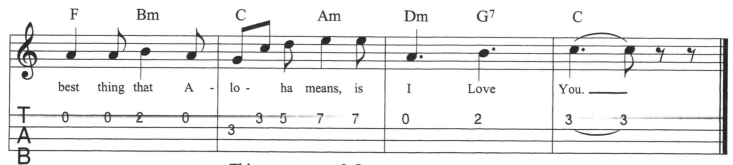

More Great Ukulele Books from Centerstream...